JEAN FOURNIER AND DAM

7 THINGS WE DON'T KNOW!

Coaching Challenges

in Sport Psychology and Skill Acquisition

MINDEVAL CANADA INC

For general information on our other products and services, please contact us at publisher@mindeval.com.

PUBLISHED BY MINDEVAL CANADA INC

WWW.MINDEVAL.COM

ISBN 978-0-9920327-0-8

First edition, 2013

Contents

Foreword

The work produced by Jean Fournier and Damian Farrow is a key development in the field of sport psychology and skill acquisition, because of the originality and subtlety of reflection based on years of experience in the field of elite performance sport in France and Australia.

As a coach of France's Women's Taekwondo team, I have always thought in terms of performance, trying to seek the most appropriate training methods. In my career, I was fortunate to meet Jean Fournier, a researcher of the French Institute of Sport (INSEP) in "performance psychology", whose methods have greatly influenced my own approach… and the results of my team. This team has, in four years, moved from eighth to second place in the world rankings and has earned two medals at the London Olympics.

This book includes a description of the methods that I have had the opportunity to apply at INSEP, as part of my preparation program. Topics such as attention and mindfulness or the acquisition of motor skills are dealt with real depth.

I have personally measured the value of mindfulness practice on a daily basis and of work on attention. This method enables athletes to be focused on the present and encourages them to accept their thoughts, without judgments, to be focused primarily on the action. The method was effective and enabled female taekwondo athletes, in varying degrees and more or less quickly, to optimize their physical potential without any additional physical training load.

The work of Professor Damian Farrow in skill acquisition and the performance gain due to what he calls "a messy practice" clearly revolutionized my approach to preparation.

All themes by both researchers shake up misconceptions about training and constitute essential input for coaches ready to challenge the "old principles" in order to progress and better realize the potential of their athletes.

Concepts such as mindfulness, attention disorder in training, anticipation or implicit training, to name a few of the topics covered in the book, are now fully integrated into my methods of preparation. The results have exceeded everything I could have hoped for, and have given me a lot of satisfaction. I am pleased that Jean Fournier and Damian Farrow, thanks to studies of great relevance, have enriched knowledge for coaches through innovative theories, giving us tools to better guide our athletes in the pursuit of performance.

Myriam Baverel

About the authors

Dr. Jean Fournier   jeanffournier@gmail.com

Jean Fournier was trained in the sport sciences. He studied sport psychology (mental training) at the University of Montreal, Canada. His Ph.D. dissertation dealt with mental training, competitive anxiety and mental imagery. Since 2004, he has worked with various Olympic athletes and coaches at the French Institute of Sports Expertise and Performance (INSEP - Paris), and with the French Golf Federation. During this time, he has provided sport psychology services to athletes and coaches in judo, figure skating, shooting, archery, diving, taekwondo, gymnastics, kayak, pentathlon, rowing and cycling. His research focuses on the effects of mental training on performance, on recovery, imagery, attention and mindfulness. Jean Fournier is an associate professor at the University of Paris 10 and the vice-president of the French Association of Sport Psychology. Since 2005, he has been Co-Editor of the International Journal of Sport Psychology.

Prof. Damian Farrow   damian.farrow@vu.edu.au

Damian holds a joint appointment with Victoria University and the Australian Institute of Sport (AIS) as a Professor of Sports Science. He was appointed the inaugural Skill Acquisition Specialist at the AIS in 2002, where he was responsible for the provision of evidence-based support to Australian coaches seeking to measure and improve the design of the skill learning environment. In this role he worked with a wide range of sub-elite and elite level AIS programs and national sporting organisations including the Australian Football League, Cricket Australia, Tennis Australia, Netball Australia and Australian Rugby Union. Since 2010, Damian has more strongly pursued his applied research interests that centre on understanding the factors critical to developing talent/sport expertise, with a particular interest in the role of perceptual-cognitive skill and practice methodology. Interacting with coaches on a daily basis in his role at the AIS has provided him with a firm understanding of what coaches like to read and the type of information they seek. He has published widely on the topic of skill acquisition and importantly has converted many academic publications into articles for a coaching audience. He is the co-author of three general interest sports science books "Run Like You Stole Something", "Why Dick Fosbury Flopped" and "It's True: Sport Stinks" and the co-editor of the text "Developing Sport Expertise: Researchers and Coaches Put Theory into Practice".

Acknowledgments

Jean Fournier would like to thank Laura Killian for her advice, Nicolas Juge for the editing, Amélie Soulard for her help with the writing, and the gang for all their comments: Marjorie Bernier, Emilie Thiénot, Emilie Pelosse, Romain Codron, Nicolas Milazzo and Alexis Ruffault.

Damian Farrow would like to thank Andy, Aimee and Jasmine for their support and the many coaches he has worked with that have shaped his thinking.

Introduction

First things first, what's the significance of the book title? Simply we are bemused by the number of self-help books out there, that all seemingly come up with the magic number of 7 rules for a more successful life, business or whatever – golf game! In this text you will find 8 rules, but for marketing purposes we have decided to leave the title as is.

This section overviews the key theoretical and practical issues that will be examined in greater detail in later chapters. Importantly, it provides a framework that the reader can continually refer to when evaluating the value of a particular strategy. This will be achieved by distinguishing between performance and learning. One aspect of athlete development that leaves all coaches uneasy is whether their player has genuinely learned the skill (psychological or physical) being coached, implying a permanent change in the player's capacity, or whether they have simply made a transient improvement that will disappear before the next practice session. This can be referred to as the performance or learning issue and understanding the difference between these closely related terms and, in turn, how they interact with different psychological and skill practice approaches is critical to creating and evaluating the approaches presented in the text.

Sport Psychology (by Jean Fournier)

Dream and reality – How to use mental imagery?

The key for using mental imagery is rather simple. Our studies have shown that the content of the images used by elite athletes varies with the goal sought. When working on a new skill, the images may be slow or filmed from the outside to understand. So, if you want to learn a move, it can be done in your head, with the same rules described in the skill acquisition chapters. If you want to reproduce a given move, the imagery speed should be similar to the real speed, the sensations should be similar to the real sensations. It's the same for the rhythm, the sounds. But if you are not trying to learn a move, nor to reproduce it to make it the same every time you perform it, then other contents are relevant. For example, when training strategy, the mental images can be modelled after real video in order to create different scenarios of attack or defence. If you want to learn how to cope with the audience, you may imagine the stands full of angry supporters clapping their hands, in order to plan your behaviours. To each function there is a mental movie.

Mindfulness: Here and Now.

Mindfulness is defined as "a state of consciousness in which one attends to present experience in all its sensorial, mental, cognitive and emotional aspects, without judging". Mindfulness enables one to focus on the present moment and employ an open, accepting attitude so as to help athletes handle their thoughts, sensations and emotions while performing, without judging. It has been demonstrated that this mental approach can lead to performance advantages as thoughts are dealt with in a manner that don't allow them to become disruptive to performance. This chapter will provide an overview of the three stage process to developing mindfulness skills drawing on some applied interventions used in the sports of golf and figure skating.

Focus: What Are You Thinking About?

In sport psychology, researchers have examined the effectiveness of different types of attentional focus and how they impact the skilled performance both positively and negatively. Descriptors such as internal and external, broad and narrow, proximal and distal or associative and dissociative have been used to describe an athlete's focus of attention when either learning a skill or during performance. With such a range of descriptions and definitions within the sport psychology literature it is not surprising that there is much confusion in the applied setting concerning what is an appropriate focus of attention for an athlete. Does one's focus of attention need to change when learning a skill as opposed to performing during competition? Does it differ if the skill is self-paced like a golf swing as compared with an externally-paced skill such as having to make a rugby tackle? These issues will be discussed and some guidelines provided to coaches.

Routines: How to Use Them?

What are the routine patterns of thoughts and behaviours that athletes engage in prior to executing their skill? Are their preferred thought patterns prior to a performance? The previous chapters have addressed the above issues in a variety of specific ways. This chapter seeks to consolidate this information and provide coaches and athletes with some practical directions of how to prepare for a performance. A variety of issues will be discussed and recommendation provided including: whether the overall length of the routine is important; what components make up a successful routine; how well practiced should a routine be and is there a need to change established routines?

Skill Acquisition (by Damian Farrow)

Skill Practice: Why Messy Practice Provides a Neat Performance?

The organisation of practice is perhaps the most influential tool a coach has to shape their athlete's skill development. There are a number of key factors a coach needs to consider when designing a practice session. Each factor can have a significant impact on how effectively an athlete will learn a new skill or reinforce an existing skill and most importantly how well their skills will stand up under the pressure of competition. The most fundamental issue that underlies all the factors that will be discussed is that skill practice does not have to look neat, well-drilled, efficient, and mistake free to be effective. In fact the most effective skill practice is the opposite, that is, it's messy, contains errors and the player's might look and feel like they are far from well drilled. This chapter discusses this issue and provides examples of how to get more from less (volume) in a skill practice session.

Developing Anticipation: How to Create All the Time in the World?

An often neglected component of fast-paced interceptive sports performance (e.g. tennis, football, combat sports) that is central to successful performance is anticipation, or the capability that enables players to commence their response to an opponent's action in advance. Both anecdotal observations and research findings have demonstrated elite athletes superiority over lesser skilled performers at predicting quickly and accurately what is about to occur. In particular the ability to 'read' the opponents movement pattern before they strike, has been identified as an information source elite players use to anticipate the likely ball or kick direction after impact. This chapter discusses recent research findings that highlight the importance of identifying the visual-perceptual characteristics of a player that may allow them to anticipate what is about to occur. Training applications are discussed for coaches of all sports who have to deal with decision-making under high time-stress.

Coaching Implicitly: Saying Less Often Means More!

A major conundrum faced by coaches concerns what is the most effective method of conveying information to learners. Traditionally, the use of instruction to augment demonstrations and practice opportunities has been at the forefront of most sports coaching programs. However a growing amount of experimental evidence investigating the role of explicit and implicit learning processes suggests that the use of instructions may be unnecessary, and in some instances lead to performance degradation rather than enhancement. This chapter will review the logic behind the implicit learning approach and then provide coaches with a number of approaches they can readily adopt and trial within their training setting.

Providing Effective Feedback: Is Real-Time Precision Really Required?

The use of feedback is another powerful tool at the disposal of a coach concerned with skill acquisition. Attention to detail in the usage of this medium is generally poor and often can be counterproductive to skill learning despite the coach's best intentions. In recent times new technologies capable of providing feedback appear in the coaching landscape almost weekly. For instance, many coaches would be able to point to first-hand experience in either using or having a sports scientist support their program with the use of GPS units, heart-rate monitors, accelerometers, skill analysis and feedback software, video applications, force plates, gaze tracking technology and the list goes on. This chapter will discuss the adoption of a bandwidth feedback approach as an underlying feedback methodology that is able to provide coaches with some clarity about how to implement feedback whether they are in possession of the latest technological gadget or are relying on more traditional verbal approaches.

1

Dream And Reality — How To Use Mental Imagery

Introduction

In 1993, I was studying the mental training strategies of elite athletes, namely judo athletes that were due to compete in the world championships, in Hamilton, Canada. One of the Canadians explained to me what how he was going to beat the Japanese competitor he was going to fight the next day. Through the use of mental imagery, he said, he had repeated his throw technique in his mind so many times that he was confident he would beat his opponent. He said, "if you see it, then it happens, what you see is what you get". Mental imagery is often used in Canada, because it is taught to coaches. The day after, this athlete quickly lost to the Japanese competitor, who apparently had another vision of the fight!

One French athlete reported a totally different use of mental imagery. 'Imagery? Doing Judo in your head? I didn't know it was called that! I've done it once in my life. I had to fight a Japanese athlete in order to win a tournament. So during the training sessions, I worked on the grip I should adopt versus him, especially, how to get rid of his right arm that prevented me from gripping him properly. But I could not physically train with him, so I imagined what I had to do when I would face him. And I repeated in my head the strategy until I got it perfectly adapted to his way of fighting. I didn't win the tournament that day. But I was able to defeat the Japanese with an unplanned throw that came from nowhere. I guess this was only because I was able to get rid of his arm, as I had planned and imagined".

A vision from the mind

Imagery is when we create or recreate experiences in the head. If it is only with image, it is then called 'visualisation'. The terms imagery or visualisation are used interchangeably. Often, images, sounds, feelings or taste present simultaneously. For example, when you imagine entering the swimming pool and the smell of the chlorine fills your nose. All senses can be used in imagery to create a virtual experience.

Imagery? First, Let me see...

Athletes are typically advised to see the perfect move, to remain composed and focused in the here and now. Really! What just in case they had planned to be beaten, highly excited, elsewhere and tomorrow. It would be nice to get what you see, but sport is more complicated than that. Mental imagery has been studied for a long time in sport psychology, so there must be something in it, even though we do not see it. It is also because we dream of a magic method in which our dreams come true. In fact, many studies have clearly demonstrated that imagining a move enhances the move more than doing nothing. In addition, imagery that supplements regular training is better for learning than practicing without imagery. In sport or in tasks with little uncertainty (basketball free throw, diving, gymnastics or figure skating), it has been demonstrated that imagery is useful to enhance an athlete's moves. In these sports, the goal is to reproduce a move without a direct opponent, or to reach a static target. Diving or gymnastics champions state that they would not have won without training with imagery. But is it useful in judo, wrestling or tennis and rugby where the opponent is unpredictable and usually not that friendly?

The content or the images (what we imagine) depends on the functions (why we imagine).

Various images are used during or between practice, and even during tournaments. For example, soccer players may imagine a match plan, as it was presented by the coach on a board, with X's and O's, and various arrows. Mental images in this case can be a single still picture, as if players were carrying a print out of the game plan in their head. Athletes practicing skydiving rehearse their free fall in 3D, feeling the wind on their face and seeing their partners moving around them during the fall. An expert golfer often visualises two trajectories of the ball before choosing the best option to result in a good location for the next shot to the green. Remember the divers before stepping on the springboard? They are mimicking theirs jumps, eyes closed, performing one last jump in their head, then whipping the water out of their body with their tiny towel. Maybe the most famous use of imagery is by downhill skiers. They are obviously seeing something when they close their eyes, and slowly dance from right to left, slightly bending their knees for every turn they imagine.

When I've asked an elite figure skater what they were visualising, they reported using different mental movies. During a training session, they may visualise the next jump right before performing it. In that case, they see the jump from inside, with their own eyes. The mental movie would come from a camera placed on their forehead. So they may notice a specific seat in the empty arena, the mark to initiate the jump, and then, how to bend the knees and ankles, when they land the jump. This is when they feel the balance, when they remember the judges, and make sure their posture is elegant. However, during a tournament, they often plan to visualise the full program, one last time before stepping on the ice in front of the audience, and the judges. In this situation, they may use a mental movie taken from the TV platform, right above the judges. In this imagery, the music is playing, the crowd cheers after each jump, and athletes make sure they have a smiley face when they skate in front of the judges.

Figure 1.1: Golfer visualising the ball trajectory.

The key for using imagery is rather simple, but we need to use it efficiently. Our studies have shown that the content of the images used by elite athletes varies with the goal sought. When working on a new skill, the images may be slow or filmed from an outside perspective for better understanding. So, if you want to learn a move, it can be done in your head, with the same rules described in Chapter 6. If you want to reproduce a given move, the imagery speed should be similar to the real speed, the sensations should be similar to the real sensations. It's the same for the rhythm, the sounds. But if you are not trying to learn a move, nor to reproduce it to make it the same every time you perform it, then other contents are relevant. For example, when training a strategy, the mental images can be modelled after real video in order to create different scenarios of attack or defence. Similarly, if you want to learn how to cope with an audience, you may imagine the stands full of angry supporters clapping their hands while you still plan your behaviors. To each function there is a mental movie.

> Do you see what I see? Rehearsing a strategy mentally does not guarantee that you'll win. The opponent or the other team might have thought of another ending for the movie.

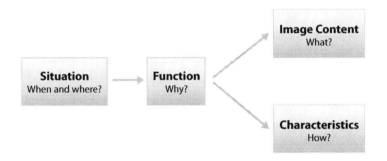

Figure 1.2: *Flow chart for designing an imagery session.* This diagram can help you to design an imagery session. It makes it easy to plan what to imagine, and how. First, make sure you know why you are practicing imagery, or why you are asking your athletes to use imagery. Of course, the function (why) is related to training or competition (situation). This figure should help you to choose the content and characteristics of imagery, if you know why imagery should be used.

Mental Imagery: Why, What and How?

What are you looking for? in defender?

You should create imagery exercises while keeping in mind the rules presented in the skill acquisition chapters, and by mimicking the drills that are really performed during training. But the content of session must correspond to your needs. To keep it simple, specify the following three guidelines when training with mental imagery.

Tell me why

Take some time to decide what you need to work on (technical issue, strategy, dealing with emotions). Set the goal of the imagery session so it helps answer the question 'WHY'. Then, you may choose the (mental) movie that corresponds to your need. In a way, you are the filmmaker, and you'll create actors to be a spectator. You've got the remote, and you can choose the channel in your mental TV, or launch another mental movie.

What's to see?

Pick up the content of the movie that you are about to make, or to play in your head. Is it seen through your eyes? Through some-one else's eyes? Or from the edge of the field? Make sure you place the camera properly. Then, set the angle and the focus: shall it be a close-up or a panoramic shot? Add the sound and the special effects: There is not limit in the budget, but remember this is not science fic-tion... You should use a content that is close enough to what you can do. Hence, the content of your mental movie answer to the question 'WHAT'.

How's that? Let's see

The quality of the picture must be set. In order to understand a new move or a new strategy, you may slow down the movie, even if you use blurry ones, but with the right feeling! So slow motion is allowed to get a grasp on what to do. If you need to enhance the rhythm of a move, then you may crank up the volume, even if you loose the picture. With the remote, adjust the pause, slow motion, contrast and brightness.

Attention Please

An imagery sequence is best when tit lasts less than 8 minutes. No need to make it longer, nor to relax before. However, you may use multiple sessions in a week, when you wake up, on the bus or after a tournament. At first, if you cannot see anything, try visualising objects, or your sports gear. Take a tennis ball, touch it, see it, feel the fur, smell it and listen to it bounce on the floor. Then try to do the same in your head. If it does not work, try one sense at a time: look at the ball, focus on the brand, then close your eyes and try to see it. You may warm up before an imagery session. Think of the place where you train, and imagine the lights, the smell, the noise around you. Try to feel the contact with your specific sports equipment. Once you are ready start your imagery session. Action!

Summary: And then what?

The more you use imagery, the better the quality of the mental images. But good quality images and the best scenario is useless if it does not match the need. The content of the images must correspond to the function. You need to adapt what you imagine to your specific needs (dealing with emotions in front of an audience, trying various tactics when facing a specific opponent, or rehearsing a given move). You may integrate mental imagery progressively into training sessions. For example, by visualising one move out of ten real moves, or one out of two, or all of them if you are injured. Mental imagery is a good way of perfecting moves without real training, and to rehearse strategies before the tournaments. You just need to adapt the content of the mental images to the goal of the training session.

Three Key Readings

1. Bernier, M., & Fournier, J. F. (2010). Functions of mental imagery in expert golfers. *Psychology of Sport and Exercise*, 444-452.

2. Cumming, J., & Williams, S.E. (2012). The role of imagery in performance. In S. Murphy (ed.) *The Oxford Handbook of Sport Psychology and Performance*, (pp. 213-232). New York : Oxford University Press.

3. Fournier, J., Deremaux, S., & Bernier, M. (2008). Content, characteristics and function of mental images. *Psychology of Sport & Exercise*, 9, 734-748.

2

Mindfulness: Here And Now

Introduction

Stress is a major concern in competitive sport. What to do with one's thoughts, emotions and sensations in competition? How to "manage" stress? This is the question often asked by athletes who do not manage to reach a good performance level in competition yet are seemingly strong in training. Stress is also used to explain why a player has lost or how a team has collapsed during a game. You may hear various comments on 'good stress' and 'bad stress', usually accompanied by cliché statements about mental toughness often followed by advice on how to proceed.

To deal with stress, several methods are available, and everyone has their own idea. However, simply wanting to manage stress lends importance to a problem. It is focusing on repairing rather that preparing. So we need to listen to conventional wisdom about good and bad stress. Many athletes believe that good stress energizes and motivates while bad stress leads to poor performance. To prevent this (that is to fix rather than to prepare), the classical solution is to relax, convince yourself that you are confident and demonstrate a winner's attitude (e.g., head and shoulders up). This solution is said to help to reach 'Flow', supposedly required for peak performance. Many athletes consider that they must work on their attitude: breathe slowly to calm down, head up and shoulders raised while using positive self talk. This belief is described in several mental training manuals. So, some athletes repeat in their heads statements worthy of Dr. Coué[1]: "Every day in every way I am getting better and better."

However, recent studies have shown that using positive affirmations might be ineffective, and inconvenient for performance. People who repeat that they will succeed may in fact be doubting: "If I use self-talk to gain confidence, it means that I'm unsure of myself". Using positive self talk may highlight the difference between the current and the desired skill level. Thus, when a tense athlete tells himself that he 'can win a tournament', unconsciously or not he is telling himself that to date he has not won, and others too can win. The use of positive statements is particularly troublesome for people with low self-esteem. Positive self-statements provide power for some, yet peril for others. Athletes who lack confidence already experience pressure to succeed. Should we add further pressure by requiring them to self-talk positively?

There is a New Method

"Every day, in every way, I have stopped talking to myself."

Since the last decade, some psychologists who had been using cognitive and behavioral therapies have adopted a new method called 'mindfulness'. Classical interventions consisted in teaching methods to fight against negative thoughts or to dispute irrational thoughts. With the new approach, psychologists teach their clients to accept these thoughts and emotions that hurt or distract them from their acting. Mindfulness-based interventions take inspiration from meditation, without the religious connotation.

The principle of mindfulness is to be aware of thoughts, emotions and feelings without judging them, and to accept them in order to act effectively. Mindfulness-based therapies have obtained good results that are calling into question previously established ideas. Scientific publications and popular books on the topic are increasingly numerous; the concepts increasingly accessible. Mindfulness-based interventions are also coming to sport psychology, but with less scientific support to date. The challenge is to change older ideas in order to ask athletes not to fight against their thoughts and emotions. Sport psychology has long embraced an active approach to the control of thoughts: Do you control your thoughts, or do you let your thoughts control you? Different themes are still hot today, such as 'mental toughness', 'stress management' or 'emotional control'. Sport psychology specialists were slow to convince athletes that they had to be mentally tough in order to be strong on the field. It is now difficult to accept that an approach that preaches acceptance is more efficient than thought control.

The challenge is to demonstrate the effectiveness of mindfulness in sport scientifically, and to popularize the concepts, as in this chapter.

Athletes who want to improve their performance do not have the same needs as patients who must undergo therapies. One of the benefits of mindfulness in sport is the facilitation of focusing in pressure situations. The goal is not to manage stress, which is inevitable when an athlete deals with a challenge, but rather to direct the focus of attention on issues that improve sport performance. To do this, the athlete must learn to focus on what works rather than seek a pleasant state (such as Flow) through fighting against 'negative' thoughts and emotions. However, we cannot directly apply knowledge from mainstream psychology to sport. First athletes seek to win tournaments, not to be cured. Then athletes are generally young people, children and adolescents. Finally, there is a major difference in the use of mindfulness itself. If the aim of mindfulness-based therapies is to avoid being lost in one's own thoughts (rumination, autopilot functioning), sport must be accomplished with the goal of automatic execution of the moves. Therefore, assessment tools and mindfulness based-intervention must be adapted to sport, and to the needs of the athletes and to their age.

At the French Institute of Sport and in various federations, several studies and interventions have been conducted to define and refine the content of interventions and to evaluate their effectiveness in sports as diverse as judo, fencing, taekwondo, shooting, figure skating, swimming, cross snowboard-cross, Nordic combined or golf. We have created a program of mindfulness and acceptance for sport. In addition, we have built a questionnaire in cooperation with the

University of Western Australia and the Western Institute of Sport in Perth, Australia. The MIS (Mindfulness Inventory for Sport) makes it possible to appraise three components of mindfulness in sport in order to build interventions and evaluate the progress of athletes.

The interventions are composed of the following steps:

1. Introduction

    (a) Presentation of the method

    (b) Evaluation

    (c) Focus of attention

2. Mindfulness training

3. Acceptance training

4. Attention training (his last issue will be discussed in the chapter on attention).

1. Introduction

a. Presentation of the method   When presenting the method, the objective is to question the certainty of athletes. Do they really want to control their thoughts and emotions, or rather to control their actions? During the presentation, we question their beliefs ("I have to feel good to play well"). We specify goals (play well) and name the opponents (the others or the environment — otherwise, athletes are fighting against themselves). This is also the time to explain that avoiding negative thoughts and looking for positive emotions are counter-productive. The athlete should understand here that simply wanting to take care of his thoughts in order to control them will give him more work. The more you think... the more you think: thought and emotion control strategies will only add thoughts to thoughts rather than remove any concerns. This presentation phase requires tact, and listening to athletes' beliefs. The worst case scenario would be to try to persuade, to lecture to death in trying to replace one belief with another one. If the athlete is not ready to abandon their convictions, it is not necessary to move to the next step. Wait until the athlete is aware of his own habits, let him understand that he is not his own opponent, that he does not need to convince himself that mental toughness is the right way, nor that he must control his thoughts to perform well. This phase is important because it is the pre-requisite for giving up a system of beliefs. However, this phase is disturbing because it does not indicate any new direction. Doubts might still be present while the athlete may still appreciate a 'confidence boost' or being able to manage their anxiety. Instead of strengthening positive thinking, increasing confidence and mental toughness, another direction is offered. What if you should not deal with your own thoughts? Could you reach a higher performance level with a lower state of mind? What if there is no link between thoughts and performance? Could a good performance lead to confidence, rather than the contrary?

Different tools may be introduced in the presentation of the method. They are useful in calling into question previous habits, to raise awareness that emotion does not precede behavior and that a thought is not necessarily responsible for the action that follows. Finally, when athletes have understood the principle of mindfulness, when coaches reinforce the work by encouragement, parents are next in line. They may have read old books popularizing sport psychology. Family and friends may provide bad advice in good faith. If on the one hand athletes learn to let go of their thoughts and on the other hand parents encourage their kids to be strong mentally, mindfulness-based programs are devalued and the results may not be as good as they could be.

b. Evaluation   Before presenting the method, it is best to know the skills of athletes. The first discussion should assess whether the athlete is aware of his thoughts and emotions, whether he accepts or fights against his thoughts, and if he knows what to focus on during competition and training. The assistance of the coach is desirable, especially for evaluating the effectiveness of focus points during training and competition. To supplement the interview or to assess groups, we recommend the use of the MIS questionnaire available online at www.mindeval.com. The MIS appraises awareness, acceptance and refocusing.

c. Focus of attention   Training in mindfulness (awareness of thoughts, feelings and emotions) and acceptance is required so that athletes may then use a relevant focus of attention. This is needed in the third step, but picking up the relevant focus of attention may start at the onset of the program. The coach is indispensable for this task. During training, when athletes are learning a new movement, or enhancing or correcting a move, what should they be thinking about? Similarly, during competition (just before starting or during breaks) what should athletes be thinking about? The coach can help the athlete to better understand efficient focus points. This work is important because it will be used in the third stage of the program. Once the athlete is lucid and accepts his thoughts (rather than trying to avoid or fight against them), he must know what to focus on.

2. Mindfulness training

In this phase, the athlete learns to know when he thinks, what he thinks about, what he feels physically and what emotions may arise. Two types of exercises may be used.

Concentration, 10 minutes per day   First we recommend concentration exercises of 10 minutes per day on breathing while sitting. This is a light form of meditation. The athlete should only focus on sensations during breathing (focus on the air entering through the nose, the sensation of stretching or relaxation of the muscles of respiration (diaphragm). As soon as he notices a thought or feeling other than those related to breathing, the athlete should gently direct his attention back to the breathing. The idea is not to relax nor to control thoughts – but simply notice the distractions and redirect attention as many times as necessary at each breath. Over the weeks of training, concentrating on breathing may be replaced by concentration on physical sensations such as posture, balance, or movements during warm up or stretching. The goal is to focus on actions (breathing, stretching) while noticing distractions. Indeed, during this 10-minute session, different thoughts, emotions and sensations will arise, which is quite normal. Rather than daydreaming and getting carried away by the flow of thoughts, the athlete should notice distractions and redirect his attention back to the task (breathing, warming up, stretching).

Figure 2.1: Player practicing a mindfulness session.

Body scan   In addition to these 10 minutes of concentration, we encourage athletes to practice several 'body scans' per day. The body scan is an exercise that lasts several seconds to one minute. It is used to probe awareness in order to quickly return to the present moment. The athlete mentally scans his body to examine physical sensations (is he relaxed or tense?), and to know what he is thinking about. This exercise helps to quickly take note of a potential loss of awareness. To put it another way, it ensures being here and now. This exercise helps monitor the flow of thoughts, thus avoiding daydreaming. It is also described as an internal 'weather report', or a periscope check from a submarine: when lost in the sea of thoughts, it makes it possible to check what's going on at the surface. To use other images, the body scan is a quick glance at the speedometer to make sure that the speed limit is respected. It is a return to reality, an alarm clock that puts you back in the present, in order to make conscious decisions — even if then, automatic moves may be unleashed. This exercise supplements the 10 minutes of concentration repeated every day. It can be done regularly at specific times during training until it becomes familiar and usable spontaneously during competition.

> *Attention! Body scan is not intended to have the athlete think during action — this could disrupt the automatic execution of movements. Processing a body scan is meant to lead to being present in the situations*

> *that require thinking or making decisions before the action but not during the execution of a move.*

3. Training for acceptance

Becoming aware of one's thoughts, emotions and feelings takes practice, but can be acquired through training. Just do the exercises as you would those in the gym. With time, athletes become more skilled at identifying what they are thinking about, as if they were watching themselves think. But the difficulty is to move to the next stage: directing attention toward a technical or tactical issue, in any case, a focus of attention that would be efficient for performance. Between the stage of awareness step and the re-focus step, athletes should master acceptance of thoughts and emotions that they are now aware of. This is really tough to do when you are a competitor. How to accept not to fight against thoughts, when 'think positive' has been heard so often? To perform the following exercises requires understanding that the opponent must be named. It is not yourself, nor is it your our own thoughts. Once this is understood (which can take time, and where a sport psychology consultant is useful) athletes must train to accept the thoughts that arise, and consider thoughts as thoughts, not as a part of themselves.

> **Labeling for Acceptance** — *Athletes may accept the thought "I'll never make it" by saying: I have the thought that I'll never make it. If the thought "I'm worthless" arises, they could accept the thought and be saying to themselves: "I notice that I have the thought that I'm worthless". By labeling thoughts, athletes may distinguish themselves from their thoughts. This helps to let go of the thoughts, rather than making them more painful by fighting them.*

Different images can be used, such as thoughts moving 'in the background', or thoughts that 'come and go'. Let's say these thoughts are present, like a pimple on the nose of a person with whom you are speaking, but that you still look in the eye. Of course, the pimple on the nose is visible, but to create contact, you look the person in the eye and make do with the rest of the face.

To train for acceptance, you can perform other 10-minute exercises. These exercises are based on the observation of thoughts without judgment, without any fixation on a given thought, nor any day-dreaming. The first exercise is to observe the train of thoughts. On each car the thought or emotion of the moment is labeled — and not the destination. In this exercise the athlete watches the train of thoughts, without stopping it or jumping on board. As soon as he stops the train, or jumps on board, he must resume the observation of thoughts and emotions. A second similar exercise is to watch the movie of his thoughts, while pretending to be in a movie theater. The thoughts are unfolding on the screen. Like for the train, the athlete is supposed to watch the movie without stopping and without acting in the film: you are a spectator of your thoughts, not an actor. The film cannot be any more controlled that when you go to a movie. Film-makers do not let the audience choose the scenarios: they surprise the spectators as your own thoughts surprise you. We do not control the emergence of thoughts. They come by surprise and leave or remain in the background. However, they pop to the foreground as soon as you pay attention to them. They must therefore be accepted, and nothing should be done to them so that they are less bothersome.

> *Remember the spot on your windshield right in front of your eyes? The more you looked at it, the more it bothered you and seemed to hide the whole road. But if you accept it, then you can focus on driving. The stain is still present AND you drive correctly. It is indeed an AND, not a BUT.*

The exercise of 'I know that'   To prepare acceptance during competition, 10-minute exercises (train or film) can be supplemented by the short exercise 'I know that'. It can be used during competition, when thoughts disrupt concentration. To be effective, the awareness acceptance and refocusing exercise must have been done regularly. The 'I know that' exercise lasts for a few seconds and can be processed over one inhalation and one expiration. During inhalation, you should be aware of thoughts, emotions or sensations that worry you, then, before expiring, you accept the thought with the word 'OK', fine, 'hum I see' or simply the word 'and'. During expiration, you focus on a technical or strategic point required for your competition. In tennis, it looks like this: (inhalation) I know I'm tense because I've nearly won on AND (expiration), I focus on serving to the backhand. In fencing it could be: I know I just missed the point, OK, I'm aiming at the left foot. Judo: I know I'm down because I'm losing, FINE, let's change the pace. In basketball, I am cross at having missed the pass AND I focus on my defensive position. Finally in golf it could be: I know I missed two easy putts, I SEE, now I align my putter head more carefully.

This exercise combines the three steps in a very short time. It enables you to be aware, accept and refocus quickly. For this tool to become effective, the three steps must be practiced, and the last step (focusing on a relevant point) must be decided with the coach.

4. Training attention

The choice of a relevant point of attention (on the movement or on strategic aspects) generally varies depending on the situation. In training it is often efficient to focus on movements (except during training which aims to improve strategy). During tournaments, or in competition simulations the efficient focus of attention point is often the result of the action (strategic issues, rather than technical ones). The methods for determining these points with regard to the situation are described in the following chapter on attention.

Summary

Importing mindfulness to sport psychology is a challenge. This method is different from before: instead of trying to control the thought, we suggest that athlete should act. The method is made of three steps. First athletes should notice the thoughts and emotion, in order to let them go — as they came. Second, once noticed, thought can be accepted simply as thoughts. Third, the athlete may direct their attention to a relevant focus. Mindfulness requires training to be efficient, so the athlete must take time to train with this new method.

Three Key Readings

1. Gardner, F., & Moore, Z. (2012). Mindfulness and acceptance models in sport psychology: A decade of basic and applied scientific

advancements. *Canadian Psychology*, 53(4), 309-318.

2. Aherne, C., Lonsdale, C., & Moran, A. P. (2011). The effect of mindfulness training on athletes' flow: An initial investigation. *The Sport Psychologist*, 25, 177-189.

3. Bernier, M., Thienot, E., Codron, R., & Fournier, J. (2009). Mindfulness and acceptance in sport performance. *Journal of Clinical Sports Psychology*, 4, 320-333.

3
Focus: What Are You Thinking About?

Introduction

The notion of 'focus' is not well defined. We often confuse attention and concentration with imagery or relaxation. Let's clarify. Focus is an engagement in perception, thoughts or movements. More simply, the focus of attention represents what we are thinking about. As it is difficult to remember what we are thinking about while performing an action, the focus of attention is related to the last thought, image or emotion created before the action. In this chapter, we propose that it is better to think before acting.

Focus can be internal or external, depending on whether we think of ourselves and our actions or what is outside of us. An internal focus of attention may refer to a movement, a rotation of the torso for example, or the position of the shoulders. On the other hand, the focus of attention is external when you think about where you want to shoot a ball.

Research has shown the importance of identifying whether the focus of attention is internal or external as this may enhances or disrupts learning and performance. Studies show that when experts think too much about their actions (internal focus of attention), it may interfere with their skill, especially when stress arises.

When performing a parallel park in your car, you usually quickly manage to fit your big car in a small parking space without any problem. However, if someone looks at you as you maneuver or if you pay too much attention at what you are doing as you park, it is likely that you will have to try several times to succeed at this same task under the eyes of your amused audience.

Attention is a much discussed topic in the world of sport. According to various researchers, thinking of an external focus produces better performance than thinking about the movement itself (internal focus). It is likely that an internal focus leads the athlete to voluntarily alter their posture or movement. Such deliberate action during the execution of a movement that is already mastered disturbs automatic motor processes and reflexes that usually control the movement. Wanting to consciously control a movement decreases its efficiency instead of improving it. Too much control kills control. On the opposite, an external focus unleashes automatic or unconscious processes. In addition, recent studies show that it is not necessary to be an expert to have our performance improved by an external focus of attention. Choosing a specific external focus of attention (e.g. thinking of a badminton racket) would be more efficient than using an internal focus of attention (e.g. thinking of the arm movement). In general, studies show that beginners do better when they focus on the execution of actions (internal focus), whereas this distracts experts who have automated their movements. Experts perform better when they focus on external things.

Controversy: Should we think of the end or the means?
For years, researchers and consultants in sport psychology have said that we should not think of the final score and even less compare ourselves to other competitors: this causes anxiety and distracts one from the task at hand. This is why focusing on the task at hand (the process, not the outcome, the means rather than the end) is a strategy that has been emphasized.

   This advice comes from research in physical education ('gym class at school'). When practicing a physical activity without competition, it is certainly good advice. However, in competition and for sports experts it is different, especially when the movements are already mastered. In this case, thinking about the outcome of a movement (e.g. where to aim before kicking a ball), seems much more effective than thinking about the gesture itself (how to kick the ball).

Paralysis by Analysis

If all goes well in training, the problem in competition usually comes from anxiety. When an athlete wants to win or when the issue of a competition is important, the athlete's focus can often change from an external perspective to an internal one. Sometimes, the athlete is paralyzed by the pressure and cannot do as well as in training. She 'chokes', she freezes. Several reasons can explain this behavior, but the most likely hypothesis is that the pressure of the situation causes anxiety which diverts attention to the execution of the movement. Thinking about the movements or the steps to perform one after the other, deteriorates the automated coordination of movements. Thinking of several internal points of attention rather than to a single external point of focus breaks previously automated skills and reduces the performance.

What do you want to do? Focus on goal, skills will get you there.

Figure 3.1: Car racer wearing an eye tracker to monitor his gaze.

However, it is agreed that it may be useful, in some cases, to think about the execution of movements like when you want to modify a relatively automatic skill or lift your technique to the next level, for example. Somehow, the expert athlete is temporarily back in the shoes of a beginner. Several strategies are possible for improving a technique already learned. It is possible, in some sports, to slow down the movement. By slowing down, you can deconstruct coordination to edit and produce a new motor pattern. In addition, the coach may decide to reduce the number of instructions given, or the number of technical points to pay attention to by choosing a single word or image that captures the essence of what the athlete has to do — rather than long instructions and several keywords. Using a keyword related to the execution of the movement can be useful if that word summarizes the intent behind the gesture. It's important that the chosen keyword does not break the whole action into steps nor focus the attention exclusively on parts of the movement.

> A **keyword** is a word or an image summarizing the most important aspect of a movement's execution. For example, in judo, one can think of the word 'shoulder' to indicate that she must completely turn her back on the opponent until her shoulders touch the chest. A single keyword avoids having to use a series of instructions. Similarly, a metaphor invites the athlete to think about the whole movement rather than just a part of it: With my laser eyes, I aim at the top right corner before the kick. In rifle, before shooting, my feet are stable as if I had roots in the soil.

When we examine scientific articles, it is apparent that it is difficult to agree on the definition of an external focus of attention. For example, in basketball, it seems to be better to think about the basketball ring at the time of the shooting, but in tennis, it would be preferable to think about the tennis racket. However, it is clear that the board and the racket are not part of the player and could be considered as external points of attention. But one could argue that the racket is an extension of the arm... And what about a footballer who focuses on the foot that hits the ball? Would he adopt an internal focus while the racquet would be an external focus? Similarly, is a golf club internal to the player? Should the golfer focus on the ball or on the target? In archery, is it better to focus on the target or the sight window, on the handle of the bow?

We have conducted studies in various sports to examine the different focus points used by athletes (see Bernier and colleagues). Our research shows that not only can the point of attention classification referred to as internal or external can be refined, but also that these focus points change rapidly. This is why it is best to deal with the last focus point that precedes action. We first improved the classification by contextualizing the points of attention (e.g. training or competition). Each situation brings a different reason for using different points of attention. Second, the finding of a rapid change of focus led us to reconsider the composition of pre-performance routines (see next chapter).

Our research in golf and figure skating allowed us to classify points of attention depending on training or competition situations. We defined focus points according to their content (focusing on the process, the outcome, the psychological or the environment), and their characteristics: the senses (visual, auditory or sensory), reality (real or imagined appearance) and intention (deliberate or spontaneous). We found important individual differences. But overall, in training situations, the focus was 60% oriented toward the process (how) whereas in competition, points of attention were 60% oriented towards psychological states.

How to Improve Focus

Regardless of the variation of these focus points in time (see the routines in the next chapter), it is important to choose the focus points that are effective in different situations. Here is how to choose effective focus points depending on the situation in three steps:

1. Find the relevant focus point for each training or competition situation.

2. Train to vary and maintain efficient focus on this point in training. It's OK to change your focus if you happen to find another more effective point.

3. Include the relevant focus point in competitive situations.

This three step process can be used to determine the content and characteristics of an efficient focus. It can be referred to during training to develop actions and strategies, and in competition to get a good result.

jumping →
contextual
ground.
skating - pushing
edges off the
ice.

Which Focus of Attention for Which Situation?

The key in maintaining an efficient focus is awareness. This implies that we should find one point, not more, to simplify and to direct attention to one direction. Attention training requires being aware of the different foci's of attention. The idea is not only to find out what thoughts are about, but also to examine the links between these thoughts and the performance that immediately follows. To do this, we must first identify situations that are typical of the actions, strategies in which competition or pressure is present. For example, a serve or return in tennis, a free throw during basketball practice, pirouettes or small steps within a figure skating solo. Typical situations also involve moments of competition, such as the start in swimming, a basketball free throw, a last dive during finals, or a difficult jump in figure skating. **It is therefore important to identify the most important situations, which often reoccur during training and competition.** In soccer, for example, it can be represented as shown in table 3.1. On the first row, the situations are listed, one per column. The second row is reserved for the focus of attention for each training situation. The third row is to note the attention to the same situations in competition.

	Passes	Dribble	Free kick	Head shot
In training	Whip the ball	Change direction at the last moment	Leaning forward	Keep the eyes open, follow the ball
In competition	Look where the teammate is running	Look at opponent's foot placement	Visualize ball trajectory	Think where the ball will land

Table 3.1: Examples of focus points in soccer.

Identify focus points   To identify focus points, we ask the athlete to remember her last thought before the start of her performance. Indeed, it is generally impossible to remember the thoughts and emotions that occur during the action. It is hard enough to remember the last thought before action. If the athlete cannot remember her last thought, we can film her and ask her to recall what she was thinking about as she looks at the video replay. You can also ask her to think aloud her thoughts, as they arise (which is a difficult task), while she practices. Sometimes memories come back more easily by imagining (or imaging) what we thought at the time of the action. Mimic is also a good way to remember.

When these methods do not work, it is possible to interrupt the athlete in training at the very beginning of her movement to ask her what she thinks. By repeating this exercise several times the athlete gradually learns to become aware of her thoughts, feelings or emotions as they arise.

It is important to some spend time repeating the exercise in different situations to clearly identify the points of attention. But these focus points may vary in the season as the action or technique improves. It is therefore important for the athlete and coach to update their focus points (using an approach as presented in Table 4.2) to see how the focus points are modified during the season, following the technical improvements and strategic progress in physical preparation.

Focus Points' Efficiency: How to Train

Finding the correct focus of attention is not enough. We must not only be aware of our thoughts (their content, their characteristics, in different situations), but also evaluate their effectiveness. Thus, it is interesting not only to record the thoughts that occur before the performance, but also the quality of the actions and the results produced.

Focus of attention efficiency: In this exercise, we ask the athlete to record for each try, or every 5, 10 or 20 tries the thoughts that arise (what do you think? How do you feel?) and the result (quality of the action or strategy? Obtained results?). The coach must contribute to this work by providing a performance criteria so the athlete can evaluate herself correctly. If it is the quality performance of a movement that is evaluated, the coach must indicate the acceptable range (height of arms, quality of the pass, timeliness, accuracy, etc.). On the other hand, if we are talking about results, criteria must be based on time, distance from the target or the gap with a good score or a competitor.

By repeating these exercises in training situations, and in competition, it becomes possible to update the table that summarizes the effective points of attention that arise repeatedly in a given sport, in typical situations.

Verification   Other exercises are also necessary to complete the work on focus points. Once they are identified, it is possible to verify their effectiveness. For example, a tennis player found that it was more efficient to think about the target when serving in competition, but that in training, thinking about his pace of action (slow then fast) when serving was more productive. Before testing this focus in competition, it is necessary to check the effectiveness in changing attention: how does work to focus on the target during training, and conversely, how efficient is it to focus internally, on a technical element, in a situation such as a simulation of competition?

During these verification exercises, it is important to note first if the attention is focused on the selected point as expected, and then if this type of attention is efficient. So the athlete must be able to answer the following two questions:

1. Am I able to keep my attention on a given point just before playing?

2. Can I assess the effectiveness of my focus point using a performance criteria?

Finally, to be sure that the efficiency does not come from repetition (habituation) during these verification exercises, it is desirable to modify the focus points from time to time to see if this impacts performance also.

A single thought isn't systematically consistent with what we look at.

The focus point represents the last thought, image or emotion before a movement. During the action, it is likely that the athlete may not be aware of his thoughts, especially if the action is fast. However, it is important to distinguish between what we think and what we look at. Players often say they have their eyes on the ball, or on the corner of the goal, just before playing. But staring at a target does not mean thinking about it. Remember your last class: you can watch the teacher while thinking about something else. Or, remember driving to your last appointment: you can set the yes on the road while imagining the questions to be asked in an upcoming interview. When working on the points of attention, it is necessary to distinguish between what is being looked at and what the athlete is thinking about.

Effective Attention in Competition

Once the focus points are specified in typical training and competition situations, and once the effectiveness of these points is established in training, it becomes necessary to use them in competition.

How to change focus points?   To change a focus of attention, we must know at all times what we're thinking about. So the work on mindfulness (see Chapter 2) is crucial. Such work allows the athlete to know when the focus changes by itself and when distraction occurs. Monitoring the change of focus and acceptance are two skills developed with mindfulness. It's important to know your efficient focus point and to be able to go back to the demands of the moment. Thus, when there is a distraction, it becomes possible to let go the thoughts and to redirect attention to a point that is efficient in the current situation. Remember that selecting an efficient focus of attention before the action allows a player to be immersed in the action. By thinking before the action, we can act during the action.

During break periods in competition, it is important to remember one's external focus of attention — especially as the pressure rises. The 'I know that' exercise (see Chapter 2 on page 33) allows noticing the pressure, to accept the distracting thoughts, to finally refocus on the efficient focus of attention.

Our whole interest in the choice of an effective point of attention lies in the use of these points at the end of your routine, just before the start of a movement or the beginning of an event. These routines must lead to an efficient focus of attention by a series of well-organized actions and thoughts. The next chapter explains how to use routines.

Summary

The focus of attention is what we are thinking about. We insist that using an external focus produces better performance than thinking about the movement itself (internal focus). Each situation brings a different reason for using different points of attention. We suggest a three-step process to improve focus; 1) find the relevant focus point for each situation; 2) train to vary and maintain efficient focus on this point during training; 3) use the relevant focus point in competition.

Three Key Readings

1. Bernier, M., Thienot, E., Codron, R., & Fournier, J. (2011). The attentional focus of expert golfers in training and competition: A naturalistic investigation. *Journal of Applied Sport Psychology*, 23, 326-241.

2. Magill, R. A. (2011). Attention as a limited capacity ressource. In R. A. Magill (Ed.), *Motor Learning and Control: Concepts and Applications* (9th ed.). New York, NY: McGraw-Hill.

3. Wulf, G., & Lewthwaite, R. (2010). Effortless motor learning? An external focus of attention enhances movement effectiveness and efficiency. In B. Bruya (Ed.), *Effortless Attention: A New Perspective in Attention and Action* (p. 75-101). Cambridge, MA: MIT Press.

4
Routines: How To Use Them?

As the whistle blew, he took the ball and headed toward the basket. Three seconds before the end of the match. He placed his feet two inches behind the line on the court. He wiped the sweat from his brow while the floor under the board was being cleaned. He breathed out slowly hearing the audience's madness. Then he bounced the ball twice, as always. He looked at the ring of the basket for the first time, imagining the trajectory of the ball and the 'swish' noise that always accompanied the passage of the ball in the net, as usual. Then he set his eyes on the back of the basket one last time, as always, before launching his ball to win the match.

Introduction

A persistent belief claims that a routine (what we do just before the sporting movement), made of the same actions repeated systematically in a given time, ensures excellent performance. The reason for this is quite attractive: if we make the same movements, we put the same (good) conditions in place and therefore, it causes a good performance. According to this belief, we should teach a fixed routine to obtain consistent results.

In fact, a routine is not solely composed of actions that can be observed. The athlete's performance routine certainly includes observable behaviors, but also all her thoughts. These thoughts and mental images are related to focus points, as presented in the previous chapter. These thoughts and images may be associated with physical sensations and feelings. Moreover, some behaviors, such as deep breathing or eye movements are not always observable. These behaviors are always the same... well, on average. In fact, they vary every time. Finally, nothing explains why putting up a sleeve before serving in tennis ensures performing a good service. Repeating ritual actions before shooting an arrow is not logically linked to accuracy in archery. A beginner may perform these rituals carefully without ever reaching the target. We must distinguish between behaviors that are relevant to the performance from those who seek to regulate emotions. This brings us back to a question raised in Chapter 2: Does the athlete wish to control her thoughts, her emotions, her performance or her routine? What is sought is a high and regular performance — not a nice routine. The routine is only a means and not an end in itself.

A regular routine is, in beliefs, supposed to be effective for sporting skills that are identical. But sports movements are never the same. Too many factors are involved — everything varies and changes. Even if the environment, the score and the opponent were identical, the athlete himself is different from one day to another. Since the task is always different, this is why it is not logical to always perform the same routine. We propose that the structure of the routine, namely the sequence of the elements included in it, stays the same, but the content stays flexible to adapt to the requirements of each situation. Thus, an effective routine should lead to focus attention to a point which facilitates automatic execution of actions and good performance.

Figure 4.1: Archers performing a routine

Routines have been studied for a long time, mainly in sports or specific activities like free throws in basketball, penalty shots in rugby and football, free-throws in baseball or putting in golf. But even in these examples, the routines are not precisely defined: we do not know where they start. Do they include the collection of information about the opponent or the field, or only the few seconds before the action? Obviously, a routine that includes strategic aspects or landmarks from the surrounding environment lasts longer than a few seconds before the rifle shoots for example. Finally, it has not yet been reported whether mindfulness would be useful in routines. We propose to add the use of the 'scan' within the routine. But first, let's explore why routines help to achieve good performance.

Researchers have explained that routines work for three main reasons. First, routines control distractions. When the stakes rise, distractions and thoughts are more numerous and more disturbing. Athletes then have a tendency to focus on themselves as their muscles tense and their heart rate accelerates. These signs are perceived by the athlete and create distractions that can be controlled by the routines. Second, routines can regulate the activation level (stress, physical arousal). Breathing more slowly, relaxing the muscles or, to the contrary, warming up physically, are routine actions that facilitate the achievement of an optimal arousal level. This is very useful especially when the practice is interrupted, or even during the course of action without interruptions (e.g. swimming, running). Third, routines are beneficial to help create automatic actions. During game interruptions, or when returning to physical activity after a break, movements are not immediately fluid. Routines can therefore be very useful for athletes to achieve a more fluid or a faster execution of movement.

Routines generally consist of three steps. The first one is a transition phase between the previous action and the next action (e.g. between two hits in fencing). During this moment, the athlete takes a short time to consider his next action or his next strategy. This reflection applies not only to events that have already happened or those that will come, but also to the physical state and the thoughts of the moment. This reflection leads to a decision phase, where a well-assured choice to direct the attention towards a point, if possible external, is made. The athlete then considers a target, or a result he wants to obtain. Finally, during the third phase, the athlete must fix his gaze on what he seeks to accomplish (grab the opponent's sleeve, aiming to reach a target, regulate a race pace or focus attention on a ball hit). The third phase is the time to move from thought to action, so that the movements already learned can be done without thinking.

From our experience with elite athletes, the structure of an effective routine should consist of the following elements, in the order listed. This structure is adaptable to different sports, but must be individualized according to the habits of each athlete.

Body-mind scan and activation management

In this first step (body scan), the athlete ask two questions that allow him to be aware of his thoughts and his activation level (What am I thinking about? How do I feel?).

Activation

When assessing his feelings, the athlete identifies his activation level to regulate it, if possible. If he is too activated to perform a fluid motion, then it is necessary to reduce muscle tension in order to reach the optimal activation level. On the opposite, if his activation level is too low (the athlete feels sluggish, flabby) then it is necessary to raise the level of activation. Relaxation or activation methods are useful at this point to quickly modulate the arousal level. The idea here is not to do a deep relaxation session, or a brand new warm-up which would be too long, but to quickly adjust the best we can to the level of activation. However, the time needed to regulate activation is sometimes too short, and it happens that athletes do not succeed in efficiently adjusting their activation level in exceptional or unusually intense situations. In this case, the body-mind scan technique at least helps to be more aware of our extreme tension so we can adapt our movement or our strategy to cope with the situation. If the athlete is not able to modulate his activation level, he can take it into account and adapt his actions.

Awareness

Observing her thoughts at the beginning of her routine helps an athlete to accept them, and focus on effective action. When taking into account uncontrollable thoughts (fears, doubts and beliefs that are unrelated with the sporting skill to be performed) the athlete is able to focus her attention on elements that are relevant to good performance. This phase is very quickly done while breathing in and out: "I know I'm afraid, OK, I think of my start". Or, "I realize that I have a lot of confidence, AND I aim at the ring".

Environment

In the second phase of the routine, the athlete may focus on the external conditions of her performance. First, all factors related to the opponent should be taken into account depending on the choices made before the competition. Thus, it is necessary to consider the opponent's fitness level, his typical attacks or his previous strategies. On the other hand, the parameters of the environment (weather, field conditions, and the crowd's attitudes) must also be well regarded. Often, changes in the weather or ground conditions change strategy to be adopted.

> Being self-aware (by performing a body-mind scan and asking ourselves two questions: What I am thinking about? How do I feel?) and being aware of the environment allows us to decide on a solution for effective action. If a fencer is lucid enough and he knows he is tensed (and that he can relax more) and that his opponent is right-handed, so he can choose a specific target and a specific attack strategy with his foil. This solution corresponds to both his current state (sensations and thoughts) and a particular strategy adapted to his opponent, during the seventh hit.

Strategic choice, ending with an external focus

Decisions made during time outs, stems from the conscious consideration of all relevant parameters of the sport. The importance of these parameters is constantly changing and the athlete's skill consists of, with experience and their coach's help, retaining the most relevant information. For example, in taekwondo, the knowledge of regulations allows the athlete to choose to push their opponent to make mistakes that are penalized rather than through direct attack. In tennis, the observation of the previous serves provides guidance on the type of service to come. In golf, awareness of a rise in temperature indicates that the ball will go further and that one should therefore adjust the power of her swing or choose another golf club. So, decisions made during game breaks depend on external conditions, which is well known — even if it is not always practiced. But the decision depends mainly on the athlete's mental state at a given moment, which is usually less practiced. This is why the 'scan' is essential in the early routine. Indeed, faced with the same situation with the same score in the same court and assuming that the opponent is in the same conditions, the player himself is not necessarily in the same physical or mental state.

> Decision making in action, rather than during time outs, is not related to the routine. We must distinguish the decision made before the action, when it is possible to make a quick assessment taking a few seconds, from the decision made in the moment (one pass, one shot) which is more automatic.

The decision that comes from the study of different choices and conditions is more easily performed when leading to an external focus of attention (make a move to the right, aim at the left shoulder, kick to the top right corner, choose tactic number 34 from our playbook). Studies have shown that an external focus of attention facilitates a more fluid and automatic execution of movements. Wherever possible and depending on the specificity of the sport, concentrating on an external (strategic) point of attention is more effective in competition than focusing on an internal and movement oriented point of attention.

> ### 'Quiet Eye': Faster or slower?
> In sports or tasks in which the objective is to aim at a target (free throws, putting, shooting) various studies have shown that staring at the target for two to three seconds before the action ('quiet eye') increases performance. However, other researchers criticize the extension of the routine this may involve. They instead recommend

reducing the length of the routine to reduce distractions. More-over, the effectiveness of the quiet eye strategy must be put into perspective when the opponent can observe the look. For exam-ple, if a goalie finds that the shooter stares at his left side, he may suspect something.

How to Develop and Enhance a Routine

Often, athletes already have a routine that is more or less complete, logical or effective. Except for very young players, athletes are gener-ally used to performing actions in a certain sequence before starting their performance. Sometimes routines are deeply rooted and diffi-cult to change. We must first identify the elements included in this routine and the order in which they appear. We then make the struc-ture of the routine evolve in order to match the succession of actions and thoughts that correspond to a more effective routine. Finally, we automatize the new routine in different situations (training and competition) to systematically reproduce it at each competition.

1. Identify the structure. Make an inventory.   To identify the structure of the routine, it is important to find the beginning. The end is easier to pinpoint, it is usually when the player hits the ball, releases his arrow or greets his opponent before the fight. But deciding on the beginning is difficult. The beginning of a routine allows the athlete to take a moment to mentally replay what just happened and to assess his state of mind. Before changing the routine, it is worth noting the current situation.

Exercise: The line   Indicate actions and thoughts above and below a line in a chronological order. Once the start of the routine is identi-fied (whistle blow indicating the penalty, the referee's calling of the score in table tennis, the choice of the next arrow, replacing the shin pads, etc.) the athlete may enter from left to right, above the line, all essential behaviors and below the line, any desired thoughts, images or keyword for the routine. Behaviors include breathing, eyes toward the target, mimics of the movement to be performed, but also all the usual small gestures that are not directly useful to performance, such as pulling up a sleeve, tightening a noose, wiping one's forehead.

Thoughts are recorded below the line and relate to lucidity (scan), the analysis of the previous move in the strategy or in the technique.

To identify key elements of the routine, you can film the athlete and ask her to clarify her thoughts as she watches her actions. Thus it is easier to become aware of the sequence of elements of the routine before changing it.

2. Content and order of the elements of the routine — from the self to the target   The observation of thoughts and actions that make up the routine allows us to rearrange these elements. Once the current routine's structure is outlined, it is desirable to place each item in its place — or the place that seems the most logical. We suggest starting the routine with a phase of lucidity (scan) and end with a point of external attention, simplifying the full routine. Starting with a scan, the athlete may become aware of his physical condition, his thoughts and emotions. To simplify the routine, you must remove all elements that are not of use useful technically, strategically or that don't help manage attention. Remember that the purpose of the routine allows an athlete to automatically perform their actions. We must simplify. A routine can be made of a few steps or phases in order to lead the athlete to the target, to the result of his action.

First performing a body-mind scan helps regulating the activation level, but also taking into account external factors. So, it is best to start with self-examination and explore the environment afterward-rather than the reverse. Once the scan is completed, the sequence of thoughts must be ordered. It is best to first address the strategic issues to complete the routine by orienting the attention toward the target. Depending on the sport, diving for example, it may be necessary to mimic the movement to be performed or to imagine it at the same time. In form production sports (diving or gymnastics) recalling the movements through mime or imagery can lead to a focus on the action rather than the result. We must be careful to complete the routine by focusing externally, in a simplified way.

In form production sports (e.g. figure skating, trampoline), it is preferable to choose a single focus point (or a single mental image) that summarizes the movement rather than a succession of points of attention. Indeed, too many focus points may break down the movement, making it less fluid, less automatic. Expert coaches usually choose a single image, sensation or metaphor that summarizes the entire action, which avoids its deconstruction. So, it is best to choose as few focus points as possible.

For example, a fencer may first perform a body-mind scan to become aware of his sensations, and then analyze the previous hit to choose the next one. He can then mimic what to do, or picture it mentally not to show it to his opponents. He'll then be able to regulate his activation level (breathing, walking, etc...) and finish the routine focusing — not on the action to be done, but on the target to be hit (his opponent's left hand).

Note that the choice of the order of the routine's elements is 'formal'. It is used to give structure, to organize the moments that precede action, albeit this structure is sometimes different. Among experts, attention alternates between the outside to the inside, back and forth quickly. Our advice is generally to adopt a chronological structure of the routine, starting from the athlete (internal focus) and finishing to the target (external focus). However it is inevitable that the focus alternates between the target and the means (actions) required to achieve it.

3. *To automate*   Once the new routine is set (simplified, and reordered from the self to the outside or the result of the action), the athlete should try it during training. When the new routine structure is validated and considered effective, it is time to learn it 'by heart', in order to successfully perform it — when it counts! Indeed, in training situations aiming at developing a gesture or the part of a movement, the complete execution of the routine is not necessarily required. By contrast, as soon as a challenge is present as in competition or in training situations under pressure, then the routine must be performed: when the points are recorded, routine counts.

Until the next competition, athletes can use imagery and simulate the routine to make it more 'natural', automatic. The coach who observes an athlete must know at least one of the routine elements (action) to assess the presence of typical routine. The athlete must inform his coach of the visible action from the outside indicating that the routine is being performed. In badminton, it may be the moment the player sets eye on the cap of the shuttlecock. For a kick, it could be to place the ball's valve toward the target, or to take 5 steps. Whatever typical gesture (or deep breathing), it is important to know the small, visible action, indicating that the routine is done.

4. Training with distractions and pressure   Once it is automated and well learned, the routine must be integrated in stressful or distracting situations. It's not enough to train, we must train with stress. So, the coach can create situations that force athletes to think of themselves and their movement so they perform their routine with real distractions. To achieve this, we must choose situations that especially hinder the athlete. For example, a partner can whisper in his ear the reasons why the athlete could fail. The later should upset the athlete who will have to use his routine to refocus his attention on the point that will allow fluid execution under stress. The coach can stop the practice and ask all partners to observe and judge the quality of the athlete's actions. Visible cameras can record parts of the training that will be analyzed in public. Test results in training can be displayed for all to see. Finally, you can choose to have difficult actions performed with a single try, when the athlete is tired, at the end of training, and when it's more difficult for him to think straight. Whatever the means, it is important to choose the situation that will potentially distract the athlete.

Summary

Routines are a very effective tool in sport psychology. They help focusing attention to a relevant point, making the move smooth and efficient. To perform a routine properly, work on the routine structure is essential. But the routine also depends on the use of simple mental skills such as relaxation, imagery or identification of focus points. Therefore, the routine stands as an advanced tool based on easier psychological skills that require training in order to be mastered.

Three Key Readings

1. Vickers, J. N. (2007). *Perception, Cognition, and Decision Training: The Quiet Eye in Action.* Champaign, IL: Human Kinetics.

2. Singer, R.N. (2002). Preperformance state, routines, and automaticity: What does it take to realize expertise in self-paced events? *Journal of Sport & Exercise Psychology*, 24, 359–375.

3. Mesagno, C., & Mullane-Grant, T. (2010). A comparison of different pre-performance routines as possible choking interventions. *Journal of Applied Sport Psychology*, 22, 343–360.

5

Skill Practice:

Why Messy Practice Provides A Neat Performance

Introduction

I was invited to observe and comment on the effectiveness of a basketball coach's practice session. At the conclusion of the session I
started my review by asking the coach how he felt the session had
went. He commented on how pleased he was with how well drilled
the players had become. They moved with military like precision
from one drill to the next, all players knowing their role in the drill
and moving from one cone to the next without the need for coach
direction. He felt the content of the drills were also good — the players received plenty of practice repetitions of each skill practiced be
it passing, dribbling or shooting. For instance, in the 10 mins allo-
cated for free throw shooting practice the players were able to make
approximately 50 practice attempts — in the coach's words "really
drilling the players muscle memory of free throw shooting". Similar,
drills were completed for passing, for example players completed a
5-min block of passing in pairs before progressing into a drill where
the groups of three players passed the ball in a choreographed pattern known as the 3-man weave from one end of the court to the
other. The coach was particularly pleased with the success of the
practice session. Free throw shooting percentages were high and

hardly a ball was dropped in the passing drills. At this, stage it is probably worth asking why the coach had invited me to observe, after all his players' were practicing well. Interestingly, their win-loss record was not so good, for some reason the players were not transferring their practice form to the competitive setting. This chapter is focused on why this was the case.

The organisation of practice is perhaps the most influential tool a coach has to shape their athlete's skill development. There are a number of key factors a coach needs to consider when designing a practice session. Each factor can have a significant impact on how effectively an athlete will learn a new skill or reinforce an existing skill and most importantly how well their skills will stand up under the pressure of competition. The most fundamental issue that underlies all the factors that will be discussed is that skill practice does not have to look neat, well-drilled, efficient, and mistake free to be effective. In fact the most effective skill practice is the opposite, that is, it's messy, contains errors and the player's might look and feel like they are far from well drilled.

Practice Variability: Repetition Without Repetition

There is a popular coaching adage "practice makes perfect". Skill acquisition practitioners have a different mantra, "repetition without repetition". That is, it's not the repetition of an identical movement pattern over each practice opportunity that generates skill learning, rather its practice approaches that force a performer to adapt their technique as required to achieve a consistent outcome goal. Interestingly, it doesn't seem to matter whether the skill is closed and self-paced such as a basketball free throw or open and subject to opposition pressure such as passing to a team-mate, the benefits of adding variability to the practice drill are equally valuable.

This suggestion to encourage adaptability through variability can often be misunderstood when predominantly closed skill sports such as swimming, rowing, and golf are considered. In such sports it is argued that having stable and reproducible technique is critical to performance success. How could exposing a golfer's swing to practice variability be beneficial, surely it would make more sense to practice the skill in exactly the same manner each time? However, the available skill learning research gives us confidence that there is much to be gained by exposing both closed and open sports performers to practice variability.

If we accept that there is enough scientific evidence to suggest we need to practice our skills variably, the next challenge is to determine the appropriate amount of variability. Practice variability can be created in many ways with one of the most researched and successful methods through the application of a blocked or random practice approach. Put simply, practicing in a blocked or random manner demands differing amounts of mental effort from the learner. It has been found that the greater the mental effort a learner uses when learning a skill the better the resultant learning. Random practice involves alternating between two or more skills or variations on each practice attempt. For example, our basketball players may perform one free throw repetition and then one passing repetition and then repeat this process, free throw, pass, and so on. Neither the free throw nor the passing action is practiced repeatedly by itself. Alternatively, blocked practice involves practicing one skill continuously for a set of practice attempts before practicing another skill. For example, as described in the introduction 50 free throws were completed in a block before a passing drill was completed again in a block. All free throws were completed before performing any passing drills. Research has found that blocked practice leads to better performance of the skills in the short-term compared to random practice. Again this would explain the basketball coach commenting on how "well drilled" his players looked in training – rarely dropping a pass. This would seem logical due to players being able to get into the 'groove' on a given skill during a practice session. However, when the skills are examined over the longer-term or when transferred to competition like settings to determine whether the training performance is permanent, random practice produces improved retention or learning of the skill.

An applied research study by Kozar and colleagues (1994) examining the basketball free throw shooting accuracy of an NCAA Division 1 men's team in practice and the game highlights the importance of this issue. Players were found to shoot an average of 7-8 shots in a row each time they practiced the skill relative to the game where either 1 or 2 shots in a row. Practice free throw accuracy was 74.5%, compared with game accuracy of 69%. However, when the first 2 free throws in practice were analysed separately the accuracy was 69.8% or the same as the shooting accuracy in the game. These data highlight the importance of spacing repetitions to maximize practice effectiveness. Re-considering the basketball coach's use of a 10-min block of 50 free throw repetitions highlights a possible reason for his team's lack of performance success. Altering how the skill repetitions are completed does take some planning. Instead of simply allocating a 10-min period of shooting practice, the coach would need to find some 25 opportunities within the practice session to go and complete two practice attempts to gain the same amount of practice repetition. Two points are important here: 1) practice repetitions completed in this more specific manner have more value than blocked practice repetitions hence one may be able to practice slightly less 40 rather than 50 repetitions and yet still reap the benefits; and 2) such practice organisation simply requires attention to detail and the coach to use their imagination. For example each time a break between drills is called players could immediately go and shot two shots before changing drills — you will be surprised how easy it is to gain a suitable amount of appropriately spaced repetition. It's also well worth the effort as the amount of transfer from practice to the game depends on how closely practice conditions resemble the game.

The reasoning behind these paradoxical effects where blocked practice leads to superior practice performance but poorer learning than random practice, can be explained by the relative amount of mental effort generated by each practice approach. The need to constantly switch between different skills in a random practice schedule is suggested to create higher levels of mental effort than a blocked practice approach as the basketball player is forced to more actively process the skill requirements each time they practice the skill whereas in a blocked practice schedule the learner can "switch off" after repeating the same skill a few times in a row.

While the previous explanations make it clear that random practice generates more learning than blocked practice, the characteristics of a learner and the purpose of a session impact on the application of the practice schedules in a practical setting and influence how much variability is enough.

Characteristics of the Learner

The skill level and experience of a learner has been found to have a major impact on the usage of random or blocked practice. Specifically, beginners who have no experience or little skill in the tasks to be practiced benefit more from blocked practice than random practice. It argued that beginners need the opportunity to get an idea of the movement and establish a basic movement pattern before engaging in random practice. Blocked practice provides this opportunity as the learner can reinforce a desirable outcome or correct an error from the previous practice attempt without the interference of having to change to a totally different skill. This is logical if we consider the amount of mental effort a beginner applies to the learning of a new skill. To increase that effort by introducing a random practice schedule would only cause an overload on a beginner's limited processing capacity. However, once a basic movement pattern has been established the learner should then be exposed to a greater amount of challenge so that the mental effort required is increased. Therefore intermediate and advanced level performers can benefit more from a random practice schedule than a blocked practice schedule.

Skill Level	Skill Type	Practice Approach
Beginner	Closed	Blocked
	Open	Blocked
Intermediate	Closed	Random
	Open	Blocked
Advanced	Closed	Random
	Open	Random

Table 5.1: Examples of the interaction between skill level, skill type and suggested practice variability approach.

It's Not Black and White in Application

Coaches should also be mindful that the practice schedule itself can be manipulated between the extremes of pure random or blocked practice. Although the research has typically investigated changing skills after every trial (random practice) or completing large blocks of trials on the one skill before changing (blocked practice), there are alternatives. For example, it may be desirable to provide a practice schedule that alternates between two different skills or variations after every 5–10 practice repetitions rather than on every trial, therefore reducing the interference slightly. For example, referring back to our basketball example, given that free throws in competition are usually awarded in pairs — it would make sense to provide athletes with two repetitions before switching to another skill. Likewise the usage of skill circuits to practice a number of tasks within the one session in blocks of short time periods may be beneficial. Matching the practice schedule difficulty to the current performance of the athlete is also a valuable approach. This can be achieved through application of the win-shift / lose-stay strategy otherwise known as the popular basketball shooting schoolyard game called "Round the World". In Round the World, the aim is to move around the basketball key from spot to spot in as few shooting attempts as possible. If a player successfully shoots a basket they progress to the next spot around the basketball key (in other words if they win they shift). If they miss, they stay at the spot where they missed and can't progress until they are successful (or lose-stay). Such an approach produces either random or blocked practice dependent purely upon the athlete's performance.

Summary

- Increasing the amount of practice variability is linked to more effective skill learning particularly as a performer progresses beyond the stage of a beginning skill level. This is because it increases the amount of mental effort a learner has to devote to skill learning.

- There are many ways to create enhanced practice variability with the organisation of practice repetitions into either blocked or random schedules a common approach.

- Coaches and athletes tend to "block" skill repetition far more than is necessary for skill learning. A useful indication on when it is time to increase practice variability is when performance plateau's as defined by a number of successful repetitions in a row this is an indication to switch skills or increase the variability within the current skill being practiced.

Drill / Activity Name	Description	Level of Mental Effort
Blocked Practice	Skill practice is completed in blocks e.g., 10 kicks then 10 dribbles of a soccer ball completed separately.	Low
Variable Practice	Variations of one skill are practiced e.g., hitting a wedge golf chip with height then as a bump and run.	Moderate
Random Practice	Skill practice requires switches between more than one skill e.g., one basketball free throw repetition and then one pass and so on.	High
Performance Dependent Practice	The switch from one skill to another is determined by a learner's performance. E.g., if the golfer makes the putt he moves to a new distance from hole but if he misses he repeats the same putt.	Moderate: Effort dependent on learner's current skill level
Skill Circuits	Tabloid activities where there are a variety of skills required e.g., 1-min practice at 4 different stations each focusing on a different skill (i.e. basketball shooting, dribbling, passing, ball handling).	Moderate: Depends on amount of time (and reps) completed per circuit
Matchplay	All skills are required as demanded by the game context.	High

Table 5.2: Examples of different ways of manipulating the level of mental effort required for a learner through practice organisation.

Three Key Readings

1. Davids, K., Bennett, S., & Button, C. (2008). *The Dynamics of Skill Acquisition*. Human Kinetics.

2. Guadagnoli, M. (2007). *Practice to Learn. Play to Win*. Ecademy Press.

3. Patterson, J.T. & Lee, T.D. (2008). Organizing practice: The interaction of repetition and cognitive effort for skilled performance. In Farrow, D., Baker, J., & MacMahon, C. (Eds.) *Developing Sport Expertise. Researchers and Coaches Put Theory into Practice*. (pp. 119-134). London: Routledge.

6

Developing Anticipation:
How To Create All The Time In The World

Introduction

Shooting percentages, measures of technique, and fitness test scores are often used as a means of distinguishing elite athletes from their lesser skilled counterparts. However, there is also a less obvious quality that can often even separate two elite players. Anticipation or the ability to "read the play" is the capability that enables players to commence their response to an opponent's action in advance. Team sport coaches describe it as the player who is a good driver in heavy traffic. The basketball player who seemingly knows what's going to happen two passes before the ball is passed; the racquet sports player already moving into position before their opponent has hit the ball; or the judo master evading an opponent's move and counter-attacking. While these players may not always appear the fastest around the court, their ability to accurately forecast a games future means they always seem to have all the time in the world. While such anticipatory skill appears easy for athletes like Roger Federer, for mere mortals it's more like reading Latin.

Both anecdotal observations and research findings have demon-strated elite athletes superiority over lesser skilled performers at predicting quickly and accurately what is about to occur. Different sources of information have been identified in sports depending on the specific dynamics of the sport. For instance, in racquet and combat sports the ability to 'read' the opponents movement pattern before they strike has been identified as an information source elite players use to anticipate the likely ball/kick direction before impact. Whereas in team sports, while an opponent's movement is important, the capacity of a player to understand structured patterns of play that typically occur throughout the game is equally critical.

This chapter discusses key research findings that highlight the importance of identifying the critical opponent cues and patterns of play that may allow a player to anticipate what is about to occur. Once the important information sources have been identified and discussed, training applications are discussed for coaches of all sports who require their players to make effective decisions under high time-stress.

Understanding Interceptive Actions

While it is easy to get carried away with the ball velocities that professional tennis players are capable of generating on serves and groundstrokes, it's those on the receiving end that are really demonstrating some speed. If we look at the radar, many of the world's top male players are successfully hitting their first serve in excess of 200 km/h. Although "Hawkeye" reveals that such serves do slow down by approximately 50% on their 23.77-metre journey to the opponent's end of the court, the demands on a receiver are still immense.

In real terms the receiver has approximately half a second to come up with a stroke to avoid being 'aced'. By completing some rough mathematics we can see that the best receivers need to know their sums. If we subtract 400 milliseconds for the time it takes to complete a forehand or backhand return swing and around 100-200 milliseconds for messages to travel from the brain to the muscles, one can see that there is little to no time left for the player to decide where the serve is going and what shot to hit. Therefore, if a 200 km/h serve is to be successfully returned, the player has to make a decision and begin shot preparation before the ball has even left the server's racquet! So how do they do it?

Through the use of various experimental techniques such as the use of customised goggles that provide visual snapshots of a server's action (see Figure 6.1), sports scientists have been able to determine what particular signals (cues) receivers tend to rely on to successfully predict the direction of a tennis serve. The test conditions for this research required players to attempt to return the serve despite never seeing the ball's flight after contact with the racquet. Hence, they were required to rely purely on cues before racquet-ball contact. For example, a receiver may only see the ball toss portion of the serve, with the remainder of the service action being visually occluded. The logic behind such an approach is that if a receiver's performance is above that considered a guess then the player must be using information from the ball toss to assist with their service prediction. Comparisons between highly skilled tennis players and lesser skilled players commonly reveal systematic differences in the information used to anticipate service direction. The most significant finding being that highly skilled players are able to accurately predict or move in the correct direction to return a serve some 300 milliseconds before the serve is actually struck!

Specifically highly skilled tennis players rely on pre-contact information sources to successfully predict service direction; in contrast, lesser skilled players rely on ball flight information. Accordingly it is recommended coaches educate players about the unique mechanical features of the service action as they relate to service direction. For example, the racquet on its upward swing prior to the hit comes much closer to the head when the serve is hit to the right than when it is directed to the left. Despite occurring late in the service action and at high speed it seems that expert players in particular are able to use this information to predict service direction.

These findings specific to the tennis return of serve situation are typical in a wide variety of interceptive actions. For example, goalkeepers attempting to intercept penalties in football and handball or combat sport performers reading likely attacking moves of an opponent. In each case while the advanced information is sports-specific, the overriding observation is that more skilled players in each of the sports investigated are attuned to earlier occurring information emanating from the mechanics of their opponents action. Coaches and elite performers in these interceptive sports are often aware of what these advanced cues are, yet ironically it's not often coached to developing athletes (but more on that later).

Figure 6.1: *An example of occlusion technique for the tennis return of serve.* The goggles worn by the player are remotely controlled to occlude his vision at selected moments during the serve-return sequence.

One Step Ahead! Importantly, elite performers in these interceptive sports are those that strive to stay one step ahead of their opponents by trying to disguise the cues that may allow an opponent to anticipate an outcome. So next time you watch Federer and co. send one down and the ball swings to the backhand or the forehand, we bet you may struggle to see any difference in his technique. In addition to the blistering speed, the truly great performers also attempt to create what magicians refer to as 'misdirection'.

What's Chess got to do with Team Sports?

The capacity of a performer to recall or recognise a structured pattern of play (typically called pattern recall/recognition) was first investigated in the game of chess. Research was able to demonstrate that chess grandmasters were able to sum up a board in one quick glance. Provided with 5 or 10 seconds to look over a specific chess situation the best players could accurately recall the exact location of 90% of the pieces. Lesser skilled players could only remember 50%. The researchers concluded that the grandmasters could "chunk" the pieces on the board into, fewer, larger chunks of information that were more easily remembered and subsequently recalled to produce the required pattern. Much in the same manner as how we all remember frequently used telephone numbers as one block of numbers rather than its individual numbers.

Sports science has demonstrated that elite team-sport decision-makers also possess the analytical mind of a chess master. For example, research has identified that elite players have developed the ability to rapidly recognise and then memorise patterns of play executed by their opponents. Importantly, this capability to recognise opposition team's attacking or defensive patterns is not because the elite players have a bigger memory capacity than the rest of us. Rather their memory of sport-specific attack and defence strategies is simply more detailed than ours and can be recalled and used in a split second.

Watching a team-sport like basketball or rugby is a classic example of watching a continuously changing pattern. Interestingly, while the pattern may look meaningless to the untrained eye, that is, 10 or 30 players sprinting and dodging in all directions, to an expert player (or coach) it can all look completely logical and can inform them in advance as to where the ball is about to be passed. This is obviously quite a useful skill to possess if your job requires you to intercept as many opposition passes as possible — just ask Australian basketballer Pat Mills or French rugby star Frédéric Michalak. The common method to examine this recall capacity is to present players with video-footage of typically occurring game situations. The player view the situation (pattern) until it is strategically occluded (blacked-out or paused). Players are then required to recall the attacking and defensive structures of the two teams by plotting the location of each player as they had last seen them in the video-clip on a blank template of playing court or field (see Figure 6.2). On average the skilled players accurately recall the location of 60-80% of all those shown on video. In comparison, lesser-skilled performers recall significantly less players in the presented scenario.

Good game skill. With video.

Figure 6.2: *An example of pattern recall task from the sport of Australian football.* The player is required to position the "o" and "x" icons where he last saw the players on the field before the screen was occluded.

A range of experimental approaches have been used to explain this phenomenon. Perhaps the most insightful from an applied perspective is the information generated from the use of visual gaze recording techniques. As the name suggests, gaze recording/tracking logs where an athlete looks as a pattern of play unfolds. Gaze is considered an insight into a player's attention and a measure of what is visually important for a performer to attend to in a specific situation. These gaze behaviours are then reported in regard to their frequency, duration and order. Again while the findings are somewhat sport-specific, generalizable features include the observations that skilled performers detect similarity across patterns of play based upon structural relations (such as the tactical significance of relations between players), whereas less-skilled players depend on more superficial elements such as the ball's location. Skilled players appear to fixate gaze centrally and use peripheral vision to extract information from the positions and movements of players. Furthermore, variation in the number of players involved in a pattern of play influences the resulting visual search rate variables. For example, it has been demonstrated in offensive football scenarios, a smaller number of fixations and longer fixation duration is employed in 2 vs. 1 and 3 vs. 1 situations relative to those where there are more attackers and defenders.

Anticipation is Made Not Born!

Listen to sport commentators discussing any fast-paced ball sport (e.g. tennis, football, hockey), and you will hear them observe that the speed of the game has increased. Numerous reasons have been cited for this change of pace, in particular improvements in equipment technology and training approaches have created faster player movement and higher ball velocities. A classic example frequently discussed is that tennis players now consistently serve the ball faster and more accurately than ever before. Many of the elite male players in the world successfully hit their first serve in excess of 200kph. While rule changes are often suggested as a means of restoring the balance between server and receiver, another solution maybe far simpler. Perhaps players need to improve their anticipatory capabilities through a more thorough understanding of relevant time-stressed situations in their sport that require fast decision-making. In other words, players need to develop the ability to buy themselves time when there is very little time available.

However, even if a player is willing to develop their anticipatory skill often they don't get the assistance one might expect from a coach. A common exclamation of many coaches is that good decision makers are born and not made. They conclude this quality can't be coached. To me, this is the excuse of a lazy coach! While there will be always be players who are more naturally talented than others, all can improve their reading of the play with practice. The remainder of this chapter provides a number of training approaches that have been demonstrated to improve anticipatory skill.

The most important method to develop anticipatory skill is simply to play the game. The more games you play the more likely you are to become accustomed to specific attacking and defensive strategies and develop an understanding of where the ball will be passed. Good coaches draw their player's attention to advance information that is useful, further they demand players "bring their brain to training" rather than simply go through the motions. This is reinforced by the drills and games the coach implements with his players. For example, a common basketball drill is the 3 man weave where the ball is passed in a specific sequence as 3 or 5 players charge down the court. While this drill looks impressive when completed effectively, it does nothing to develop the players' decision making skills as it contains no opposition. The simple introduction of 2 defenders into this drill would enhance the decision-making skills of the players as they now need to choose when and who to pass the ball to and in so doing read their opponent's movements.

Off-field practice is becoming as significant as on-field practice in many professional sports. Referred to as perceptual training in the scientific literature, video sequences, computer games and even virtual reality applications are all available to present players with exposure to different decision making scenarios. While space prohibits a complete discussion on this method the key points are as follows. The key advanced information known to be important to a particular scenario needs to be presented in the training simulation. The most common approach requires players' to predict what to do next when watching a sequence of play that is frozen at a critical instant. For instance, vision of a basketball game is shown and as the basketball guard is about to make a decision the footage is paused or occluded and the participant is required to put themself in the player's shoes and determine where the ball should be passed, shot or dribbled. Further, it is important to get the players to feel as though they are under the time pressures they would experience in a competitive setting. The most effective method for recreating this time-stress in perceptual training programs is to occlude the vision of the scenario as soon as the critical information/cues have been presented. For instance, a soccer goalkeeper viewing an opponent completing a penalty kick only see's the vision of the kicking action up to the point of foot-ball contact at which time the video sequence is occluded or paused. This selective editing creates time stress as it forces the goal-keeper in this instance to attend to early occurring information to guide the decision making response. A common observation made by players after experiencing such training is that when they then ex-perience similar situations in the physical or competitive setting they feel like they have more time. This is obviously the effect the training aims to achieve and is due to forcing the performer to make decisions on the basis of earlier occurring information rather than relying later occurring information such as the ball's flight.

While the above training approach may sound logical, not only do some training methods not systematically manipulate this advanced information they don't even present sports-specific vision. Too often news articles refer to a professional club using so-called "vision train-ing" programs that purport to develop sport-specific decision making skills through the presentation of programmed sequences of flash-ing lights on a computer screen. The lack of sports specificity, render such programs as useless in the development of decision making skill.

Develop a checklist of any key movement pattern information sources that may be predictive of what an opponent is likely to do. For example, rugby coaches often cite the importance of watching an opponent's hip movement when preparing to tackle them. Most importantly, players should be coached to understand the relation-ship between the various movement pattern characteristics and the likely resultant player movement or ball direction. The use of video footage shot from the player's perspective (e.g. a tennis server filmed from the perspective of the receiver) which is then paused at various points before contact has proven a useful means of training a player's understanding of movement pattern kinematics.

Another key anticipatory information source is probability information such as an opponent's favourite kicking side, dodging direction or service location. This source of anticipatory information is vital at the elite level and requires close examination of an opponent's behaviour in different situations in order to identify particular idiosyncrasies or tactics used for disguise and/or deception in a given time-stressed situation. Video review of particular players and teams is the most common means of establishing a database of this type of information.

Summary

Anticipatory skill is a vital component of elite performance in time-stressed sports that require interception such as tennis or combat sports as well as team-sports that require the reading of the play such as hockey and football. While scientific evidence has for some time demonstrated the importance of this performance component many coaches have not attempted to systematically develop it as they believe players either have it or they don't. This chapter has provided some evidence highlighting what the key advanced information sources are for various sports but equally importantly that this capacity can be developed on or off the court/field of play through systematic training that forces players to learn the link between advanced information and the resultant action of their opponent.

Three Key Readings

1. Abernethy, B., Wann, J., & Parks, S. (1998). Training perceptual motor skills for sport. In B. Elliott (Ed.), *Training for sport: Applying sport science* (pp.1-68). Chichester: John Wiley.

2. Farrow, D. & Raab, M. (2008). A recipe for expert decision making. In Farrow, D.,Baker, J., & MacMahon, C. (Eds.). *Developing Sport*

Expertise. Researchers and Coaches Put Theory into Practice. (pp. 137-154). London: Routledge.

3. Williams, A.M., Ward, P., and Smeeton, N.J. (2004) 'Perceptual and cognitive expertise in sport: Implications for skill acquisition and performance enhancement', in A.M. Williams and N.J. Hodges (Eds.) *Skill Acquisition in Sport: Research, Theory and Practice.* London: Routledge.

7
Coaching Implicitly:
Saying Less Often Means More!

Introduction

Put yourself in the shoes of young Louis who is about to learn the fundamentals of the tennis serve. Traditionally, his initial experience may involve seeing a demonstration and receiving instruction from a coach in the following manner:

> "Louis I want you to pick up the racquet and grip it as if you are making a fist. Now take a look at my stance. My front foot is directly behind the baseline angled diagonally into the court. My back foot is behind my front foot, about shoulder width apart, and parallel with the baseline. I'm pointing my racquet at the net and holding the tennis ball against the throat of the racquet. Importantly, notice I am holding the tennis ball in my fingers as opposed to the palm of my hand".

To progress Louis to adopting an appropriate grip and stance involved roughly six different instructions or put another way, Louis had to process and remember six pieces of information in order to prepare himself. Keep in mind, at this point he hasn't even been instructed how to toss the ball and swing the racquet to produce a coordinated movement! While there are obvious shortcuts to the above vignette such as "imitate me" it does illustrate that as a consequence of the typical skill instruction process performers no matter what the skill level very quickly acquire a large database of tips and instructions about how to perform the various skills required in their sport. This highlights a major conundrum faced by coaches when attempting to convey technical information to a player. How can I do it most effectively? Traditionally, the use of instruction to augment demonstrations and practice opportunities has been at the forefront of most coaching programs. However a growing amount of research investigating instructional techniques, specifically the role of explicit and implicit learning processes, suggests that the use of technical instruction in many cases may be unnecessary, and in some instances lead to performance degradation rather than enhancement.

Explicit learning can be related to traditional coaching approaches where verbal instruction is used to coach a performer about how to perform a skill. This process typically results in the learner consciously testing or evaluating each practice attempt. For example, "I tossed the ball too high into the air, I better hold the ball in my fingers and toss more carefully..." and so on. As a result the player is able to verbalise how to perform the skill – although it doesn't guarantee they can physically execute the skill. In contrast, implicit learning methods typically contain little or no formal instruction about the skill mechanics, yet results in a learner being able to perform the skill despite being unable to verbally describe how they do it.

Rich Masters and his colleagues (1992–current) have been at the forefront of research investigating implicit learning. Overwhelmingly, the results of such work have demonstrated that learners coached using an implicit learning approach generally learn as much as those instructed more traditionally albeit it may initially result in poorer practice performance and take slightly longer (this is a good example of understanding the nuances of learning and performance). However, a number of additional advantages have been found for implicit learners relative to those who learn explicitly. Most critically, implicit learners are less susceptible to their skill breaking down in pressure situations relative to explicit learners who are more susceptible to what is commonly referred to as 'choking' or 'paralysis by analysis'. Explicit learners are more likely to preoccupy themselves with thoughts about how they are executing the skill. As discussed in Chapter 3, as a performer becomes more skilled thinking about it can be detrimental to performance. Alternatively, implicit learners who don't have any technical coaching information swirling around in their heads subsequently are less able to corrupt their movement through over-thinking the skills' production. Interestingly, this is a characteristic possessed by elite performers when 'in the zone' or playing at their best. Other advantages demonstrated for implicitly learnt skills are that they are more fatigue resistant, more durable over time, not attentionally demanding, and independent of age and IQ.

Applied Implicit Skill Learning

By now you may be thinking of examples in your own life where you may have learned a skill implicitly. If you reflect on how you learnt to walk, ride a book or even complete your first throw of a ball it's likely you did so implicitly and hopefully in most instances are still able to perform these skills sub-consciously under pressure. To confirm the implicitness of such skills – consider what would you say to coach someone to ride a bike... Difficult isn't it! This is because implicit learning is the typical way we learn and it's only been since the advent of coaching that we have disrupted this process. While our society seems comfortable allowing infants and young children to learn various skills implicitly it is also apparent there seems to be some arbitrary moment in our development where society deems it's important that we are explicitly coached — in many cases to our detriment. Imagine a coaching program from junior through to senior or sub-elite to elite performance that is structured around implicit learning principles.

While the above evidence supporting the use of an implicit learning approach is appealing, it's not easy or practical to simply remove instruction and expect learning to occur. The basic guideline for the design of applied implicit practice approaches is to develop activities that minimise or stop the learner from over-thinking about what they did and didn't do when performing the skill. This view of implicit learning is slightly different to the textbook/theoretical perspectives of the distinction between implicit and explicit learning where essentially it is either one or the other. From experience in order to apply this concept in a practical manner a compromise is required where we concede it is hard to stop the learner acquiring some rules about how to perform the skill. What is achievable is to minimise how many rules they develop and restrict the opportunity to process them. A number of specific practice methods have been developed and examined experimentally that meet this aim. I will review them below and provide examples from a variety of sports.

1. EXPLAIN THE SKILL REQUIREMENTS BY ANALOGY OR METAPHOR so that the need for explicit verbal information is minimized has been demonstrated to be one of the more successful applied implicit learning approaches. Most sports are full of good examples of analogy learning (see Fronske, 1997 for examples). For instance, referring back to the tennis serve vignette, asking players to "cut their toes with the racquet" and then "throw their racquet at the ball" paint two images that may summarise many elements of the service action. Similarly, asking a player to toss the ball as if placing an egg on a shelf conveys to them the importance of placing the ball softly into position rather than tossing/throwing the ball.

2. PERFORM A SECOND TASK WHILE PERFORMING THE PRIMARY SKILL. It is reasoned that if a learner's attention is focused on the completion of a secondary task it precludes the opportunity for them to reflect on how they are learning to perform the primary skill of interest. Secondary tasks can be selected to suit the interests of the performers but could include activities such as requiring the learner to count backwards in 3's from 100 out aloud, list capital cities of the world, sing to music on an iPod, rhyme words, or complete simple mathematics sums. In all instances it's important that the performer completes the secondary task out aloud to ensure they are genuinely committing to it. No matter what the secondary task the aim is still for them to also complete the primary task as well as possible e.g., still get the tennis serve into play with the correct action while concurrently performing the secondary task. Such practice is typically challenging, particularly in early learning and is a good example where initially skill performance may be suppressed relative to a more traditional approach. However persist as it's worth the effort!

3. CREATE PRACTICE CONDITIONS THAT GENERATE MORE ERROR-LESS PERFORMANCE. Creating an environment where the learner is always successful prevents over-analysing how to perform the skill because no errors are made. For example, practice football goal-kicking from a distance and angle where the player always scores. Once the player completes a block of successful practice attempts (e.g. 50 kicks) then progressively increase the challenge. While this approach seemingly conflicts with a number of traditional learning approaches, it seems to be particularly effective in early learning or for skilled players in a slump who are over-thinking their performance.

4. PROVIDE NO FEEDBACK TO THE LEARNER. Creating an environment where the learner does not receive any feedback about their performance (such as removing visual feedback) can create implicit learning conditions. The logic with this practice approach is that if you don't see what happened how can you over-analyse it? This somewhat controversial suggestion does have some practical support. For example, many golf professionals amass significant practice into nets where ball flight information is not provided. Similarly, Jonny Wilkinson (English Rugby Union Kicker) supposedly accumulated massive kick repetitions into a net located immediately in front of him. In both examples, the practice context removed ball flight information as feedback and perhaps decreased the amount of resultant analysis on why the ball went in a particular direction.

5. USE TASK-RELATED BUT GOAL-IRRELEVANT INSTRUCTIONS that draws a player's attention to key information or cues but doesn't directly tell him what the critical information is. This strategy is applicable when training perceptual or anticipation skills (see Chapter 6). For example, when training tennis players to anticipate the direction of an opponent's serve, it has been demonstrated that players told to predict the speed of a serve (implicit learning approach) improved their performance in predicting service direction, more than players given specific instructional tips to facilitate the prediction of service direction (explicit learning approach). It is reasoned that the implicit learning instructions directed the players' visual attention to

the important phase of the service action but let them discover the meaning of the cue for themselves.

What About Skilled Athletes?

A concern often expressed by coaches when first presented with implicit learning approaches is how could such processes work with more skilled performers who have already learned their skills in an explicit manner? While the athletes may have learned their skills explicitly, once they become skilled it is likely that they typically perform their skills without conscious control. Ironically, if a technical modification is required to a skilled performer's action coaches then tend to use explicit coaching methods where the athlete is encouraged to direct their attentional control to their movement to enable them to make the desired changes to their technique. The use of implicit learning techniques offers the potential to change a well-learned technique without the need to revert to the conscious, explicit coaching procedures where the skilled performer is required to regress back to controlling their skills more like a novice performer.

While the above is good in principle, empirically-based answers to this issue are still required. However, promisingly some evidence is emerging that demonstrates skilled players can benefit from such approaches. At this stage some tentative recommendations centre on ensuring the performer receives a high volume of implicit practice trials so that over time the player forgets all the explicit information concerning a skill's execution leaving the implicit processes to control the skill. The use of errorless learning or dual-task approaches as described previously appear to be the most successful methods to trial in this instance.

Summary

While it is acknowledged that explicit instruction is necessary on occasions, the aim of this chapter is to encourage coaches to think more laterally and consider methods that at least reduce the reliance on explicit instruction and subsequently minimize some of the negative effects it can have on skill execution, particularly in competitive situations. Remember, sometimes the best instruction a learner can receive is that Nike motto — "Just do it"!

Three Key Readings

1. Liao, C. and Masters, R.S.W. (2001). Analogy learning: A means to implicit motor learning. *Journal of Sports Sciences*, 19, 307–319.

2. Masters, R. (2008). Skill learning the implicit way: Say no more! In Farrow, D., Baker, J., & MacMahon, C. (Eds.). *Developing Sport Expertise. Researchers and Coaches Put Theory into Practice.* (pp. 89-103). London: Routledge.

3. Masters, R.S.W. and Poolton, J. (2012). Advances in implicit motor learning. In Hodges, N.J. and Williams, A.M. (Eds.) *Skill Acquisition in Sport: Research, Theory and Practice.* London: Routledge, pp.59–76.

8

Providing Effective Feedback:
Is Real-time Precision Really Required?

Introduction

Recovering from a jog on the side of a path next to the Yarra River (in Melbourne) I could hear this "beep beep beep" behind me. At first I panicked thinking it was a truck backing towards me and the driver hadn't seen me. I turned to see a squad of triathletes running towards me. The "beep beep beep" was in fact heart rate monitors signaling when the runners' had exceeded their planned heart rate for that particular effort, the coach yelling at the athletes to listen to their bodies. I then turned to the river where some rowing squads were gliding down the river. One athlete caught my attention as she was wearing video goggles as she rowed. On the river bank the coach rode beside her, filming her technique. Clever technology allowed the rower to then watch what the coach was filming in real time as she rowed (i.e., a side-on profile of her technique). In fact, these goggles are so clever that one can also provide graphical representations of force/velocity curves as the rower strokes (if the boat has the right equipment on board). The coach yelled into his megaphone to supplement the real time vision with some key cues for his athlete to adopt. By now my pleasurable post-run release of endorphins had been replaced by a mind full of questions.

What advantage is there in knowing your heart-rate in real time? Surely you can tell when you are working hard enough or not! Why was the coach yelling over the top of the heart-rate feedback? Surely he had told his squad what the beeps meant before they started training. How was the rower processing real-time feedback of her technique? Could she transpose the side-on video-perspective to her perspective in the boat? In real-time? If the information was so valuable why was the coach yelling out cues as well? Imagine if the rower's boat was wired for force/velocity curves in real time — how would she interpret this information? Are graphical representations somehow more effective than vision of technique or simply a coach's observation and subsequent verbal cueing? This chapter will discuss these issues drawing on what is established in the skill acquisition literature, as well as highlighting many of the unanswered questions. Based on the lack of a complete picture in regards to the evidence-based application of feedback, the bandwidth feedback approach will be reviewed. It is suggested this particular method offers the most practical framework for the delivery of feedback whether the coach is in possession of the latest technological gadget or relying on more traditional verbal approaches.

Figure 8.1: A coach providing feedback to an athlete using video replay.

What, if any, Feedback is Required?

As a coach it is easy to forget that as an athlete is performing a skill they are receiving a wide array of feedback. This is referred to as intrinsic feedback and includes sensory information such as how tight or stretched a muscle may feel, how fast the heart is beating, how much vibration was experienced as the club hit the ball or how balanced the movement felt. In addition to the feedback emanating from the body is feedback about the outcome of the movement, for instance, did the golf ball slice or hook, did the taekwondo kick hit the intended target, or did the gymnast complete two somersaults as required.

From a coaching perspective the starting point for determining what, if any, feedback is required is to ascertain what aspects of intrinsic feedback the athlete is aware of and using to guide their skill production and what feedback information are they not using. A typical issue is that many athletes particularly lesser skilled performers are heavily influenced by the movement outcome (referred to as knowledge of the result). For example, it is common to see high handicap golfers with set ups or stances where they are allowing for a known amount of slice. Hence irrespective of how incorrect or limited this stance may be to their long term success and subsequent enjoyment of the game, the primary feedback that captures the golfer's attention is whether the ball flies down the middle of the fairway more often than not. The longer term technical production issues which need to be addressed if the player is going to be able to hit the ball more consistently, longer and be able adapt their ball flight to different positions around the course are overlooked because of the power of ball flight feedback. In such cases, the coach's role is to direct the golfer's attention to the interpretation of other feedback information that will be of greater long term benefit. In the example used, the over-powering effect of ball flight information needs to be reduced and consequently many experienced golf coaches require their students to hit into a net immediately in front of them so that there is no ball flight information.

The dominance of knowledge of results is problematic, however so too is the related problem of performers being unable to gain useful feedback about the technical production of a skill attempt (referred to as knowledge of performance). This is particularly the case in low feedback sporting tasks such as swimming, diving and gymnastics where the athletes cannot easily see what that are doing to produce the movement but receive some strong physical sensations and effects which are often difficult to interpret. In these tasks, the coach's role in the provision of feedback is critical. The coach needs to be able to cue the athlete into understanding the relationship between a particular physical sensation and its impact on movement production. In this way the athlete has a way of making a technical correction based on feedback.

A prevailing factor that influences the nature of the feedback required is the skill level of the athlete. In general, higher skilled performers have developed the capacity to interpret intrinsic feedback more effectively. This capacity raises important questions regarding the value of many coach driven / augmented feedback strategies, in regards to the content, frequency and precision of feedback information provided relative to the skill level of the performer. For instance, it is not uncommon to see a wide variety of augmented feedback provided to athletes simply because there is a flavor of the month technology that can provide the information. Referring back to the vignette at the beginning of the chapter, just because the rowing goggles can provide a force-velocity profile of the stroke doesn't mean it needs to be presented to the athlete. Given that skilled athletes can self-monitor their intrinsic feedback, coaches need to encourage this capacity. A simple strategy such as always requiring the athlete to first report back on what they perceived before providing any further feedback encourages the athlete to self-monitor. Asking the athlete questions such as how fast they thought they went, where they thought their racquet position got to in the backswing, or how deep they bent their knees? This approach is beneficial not only for the development of the athlete's intrinsic feedback evaluation skills, but it can ensure the athlete is not dependent on the coach for feedback. After all, competitive sport requires the athlete to perform the skills without the coach holding their hand, so learning to be self-reliant in feedback interpretation is a critical part of this process.

Effective Feedback: Managing Timing and Precision

A key promotional claim of many new feedback technologies is that the device has the capacity to deliver feedback information in real time with great precision. However, the evidence supporting the value of real-time or continuous feedback is yet to be established. Similarly, the level of feedback precision an athlete requires is also a contentious issue. In both instances, while real time precisely delivered feedback may sound appealing, in fact both qualities are more likely to be at odds with what generates effective learning.

Getting the timing right

Consistent with a number of the key issues already highlighted coaches must carefully consider their logic when electing to provide real-time feedback. Most critically, will it be a distraction to the athlete processing their own intrinsically generated feedback? In general, it has been demonstrated that a learner will prioritise augmented information over intrinsically generated feedback, consequently ensuring that the benefit of real-time feedback provision outweighs the costs is imperative. Real-time feedback is a good example of a phenomenon that may indeed enhance performance but hinder actual learning (see Chapter 5). However, there are circumstances where such a feedback approach may add value to the skill acquisition process, in particular, those circumstances where the value of intrinsic feedback is low or difficult for the performer to pick-up. For instance, skill acquisition research has demonstrated that a real-time feedback device that informed gymnasts of their hip angle as they circled a pommel horse provided significant learning value. In this instance, the skill being continuous or cyclical in nature and highly complex, coupled with the feedback device being able to provide information about the critical variable that dictated movement success equated to there being value in the provision of real-time feedback. In sum, the nature and complexity of the skill being practiced are factors that need to be considered on a case by case basis when electing to use real-time feedback approaches.

What level of precision can a learner control?

Figure 8.2: *An example of the type of precision many new technologies are able to provide a performer.* In this case the angle of the club face (to a precision of .1°) when putting in golf.

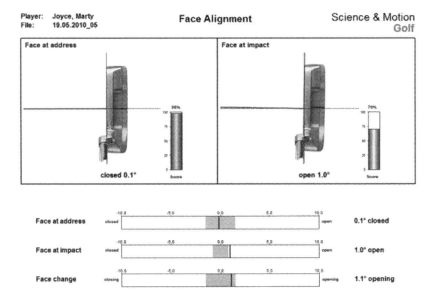

A simple way of evaluating the level of feedback precision required is to put yourself in the shoes of the athlete. As discussed throughout this chapter, there are multiple sources of intrinsic feedback information available which can then be augmented with feedback from technological devices or coach observation. However, what is the athlete's capacity to interpret and utilise all these sources of information to make a change to their skill production? Does the athlete have the capacity to control the skill to the level of precision being described by the feedback? For example, a biomechanical assessment of a backstroke swimmer's technique may reveal their arm needs to enter the water 5 degrees closer to their head. However, is the swimmer capable of detecting a difference of 5 degrees? If not, feedback with this level of precision will be redundant to the swimmer and a more general, less precise feedback cue is required. For instance, perhaps the use of an analogy that creates an image of the required arm entry position would be more beneficial and has the added advantage of promoting implicit learning (see Chapter 7). In the case of the backstroke swimmer, the use of a clock face may be a suitable analogy, for instance "your current entry position is 9 o'clock can you get your arm to enter at 11 o'clock".

Performance Bandwidths: A Useful Compromise

Perhaps the most effective means of managing augmented feedback is through the application of the bandwidth approach. Bandwidth feedback firstly requires the coach to establish an agreed range of correctness for a movement. For instance, a tennis coach may in concert with a student establish that if the racquet is swung back past the line of the shoulder on a volley then this swing is too big and feedback will be provided accordingly. However, on those swings where the racquet remains forward of the shoulder, performance will be considered appropriate and no feedback will be provided. Skill acquisition research tends to suggest the use of a reasonably broad bandwidth leads to more effective learning than more precise and in turn regular feedback. However, this issue is far from resolved and much like the issue of real-time feedback provision there will be certainly be cases where greater precision is required. The bandwidth approach offers the coach some flexibility in this regard. If a student's performance reaches a level where no feedback is required because they are constantly performing the skill within the prescribed range of correctness, the coach may elect to narrow the bandwidth further, in turn increasing the precision required which is likely to lead to the student performing movements outside of the range of correctness and eliciting feedback. Obviously one would only increase the bandwidth precision demands of a movement if this lead to a performance advantage.

The bandwidth approach offers a number of learning advantages. First, as a performer's skill level improves they will receive less feedback information from the coach, naturally fading the regularity of the feedback. One way of describing this process, is that no news is good news. Hearing from the coach less frequently becomes a positive form of motivation for the athlete. A second advantage, it that the reduction in feedback frequency as skill develops serves to reduce the athlete's dependency on feedback and increases the player's use of intrinsic feedback. Again this is consistent with the previous discussion about skilled athletes have well-developed self-monitoring skills.

Summary: Connecting the Concepts

Hopefully it has become apparent reading this chapter that there are a number of concepts that overlap and integrate with other chapters in the book. Two concepts are worthy of specific mention. In Chapter 2, the concept of focus of attention was discussed. The feedback being provided to an athlete can lead to an internal or external focus of attention and hence is important to consider. Second and relatedly, can the feedback be provided in a manner that leads to more implicit rather than explicit learning (see Chapter 7)? For instance, as discussed many new feedback technologies offer incredible measurement precision. Yet it is not well established whether athletes, particularly lesser skilled athletes, benefit from such precision. The provision of more precise information may cause athletes to be overly reactive to performance changes and in turn promote a more explicit learning approach in an effort to consciously control aspects of performance that are best left to sub-conscious control. It is hoped this chapter has reinforced that the provision of feedback is not a trivial exercise and that great thought is required by the coach to maximise the learning value of any feedback provided.

Three Key Readings

1. Abernethy, B., Masters, R. S. W., & Zachry, T. (2008). Using biomechanical feedback to enhance skill learning and performance. In Y. Hong & R. Bartlett (Eds.), *Routledge Handbook of Biomechanics and Human Movement Science* (pp. 581-593). NY: Routledge.

2. Schmidt, R.A., & Wrisberg, C.A. (2004). *Motor Learning and Performance: A Problem-Based Learning Approach* (3rd Ed.). Champaign, IL: Human Kinetics.

3. Wulf, G. (2007). *Attention and Motor Skill Learning*. Champaign, IL: Human Kinetics.

40191412R00054

Made in the USA
Lexington, KY
28 March 2015